FINGERPRINTING FAITH

52 Faith Lessons From an American Cop

Ash D. Harmon

Printed in the United States of America

Independently published in Allen, Texas

ISBN: 9798620736843

Library of Congress Control Number: 2020904341

This book is dedicated to my family who loves me,
the clergy who believe in me,
& the peacemakers who stand beside me.
I thank you.

Fingerprinting Faith: 52 Faith Lessons From an American Cop

Table of Contents

P eople always chuckle when I tell them that I had never wanted to be a cop or a preacher, but ended up being both. I can't say that I was ever really joking about it. As a kid, I had envisioned being a professional baseball player or a rock star travelling around the world, making lots of money, and being swooned over by the masses. Ironically, the possibility of a career in agriculture had entered my thoughts a time or two also. Nothing in my life ever seems to go as planned. Baseball was only a pastime for me. I didn't have any significant musical gifts worthy of rock stardom. And, well, agriculture would've bored me into an early grave.

Admittedly, I was pretty wild when I was younger. Parties, girls, and having fun had become my new hobbies. But on September 11, 2001, America was attacked by terrorists and everything changed. It seemed like every man, woman, and child in the free-world had been touched by the tragedy that was witnessed on that day. American flags waved proudly over nearly every home. People prayed together for one another. Despite nursing a gaping wound, American society became a flowing river of patriotism. It was then, during that period in history, that I was filled with an unexplainable desire to serve others, to try doing something for the good of humanity. Before I knew it I was enrolled in the police academy and became part of the 2002 graduating class at a local junior college.

The span of my law enforcement career has been as much a part of my ministry as the pulpit. Police work, and public safety in general, is a first-hand account of the human condition. There have been many people over the years who have told me that they would never have the stomach for police work. Such was not the case for me. I was half good at it and, unlike most of my prior jobs, I enjoyed doing it every day. I never knew what might happen during my shift. Some days would be boring and I wouldn't get dispatched to very many calls. Other days would be the complete opposite, making me wish I slow the world down just so I could catch up. Then, on rare occasions, there were days that were worthy of a Hollywood action film, or at least a ten minute spot on a reality cop show. Car chases, foot pursuits, domestic disturbances, barroom brawls, even the occasional shooting—we just never knew for sure how the shift would end up.

One of the most commonly recognized science associated with police work and investigation is *fingerprinting*. While you might think that fingerprinting is a modern forensic science, you'd be wrong. The use of fingerprints to verify the identity of a specific person has been around since the existence of ancient cultures. They have been found on countless documents, relics, and artifacts dating all the way back to the construction of the Egyptian pyramids. With the exception of facial recognition, it is believed to one of the oldest forms of personal identification.

The science of analyzing fingerprints is just as important today as it was in ancient times. With all the technological advances and improved techniques available to us in the twenty-first century, you'd think there'd be something more modern. DNA is invaluable, but it requires a scientist or, at the very least, someone with a highly advanced education in the field. It also takes a great deal of equipment and time to process. Facial recognition software has also improved. Like DNA, there's special equipment involved. But fingerprinting is simple. It's a fundamental form of personal identification, and pretty much any person can look at fingerprints and be able to see the differences in each one. A person's fingerprints are unique to them. At a distance, all prints may look the same. But when you take a closer look, you'll notice the features in each one are slightly different.

I can't remember exactly when it was that I discovered our faith is like our fingerprint. Although all of Christianity might look the same at a distance, a closer look reveals that our individual faith practices and beliefs are quite different from one another. Like fingerprints, tiny variations in our lives shape a perfectly unique image of faith for each of us. These variations result from personal experiences in our lives, our environment, tradition, and so on. Our interpretation of how God works in each of these things is what makes these variations unique to us. Take, for example, the death of a loved one. This is probably one of the most spiritually-challenging events that a person can experience. Now, let's look at three different examples where this event and the spiritual experience varies in different ways.

In example # 1, John learns that his wife, Sarah, has incurable cancer. She is terminally ill and her time limited. John and Sarah have spent many years of their lives as Christians and are involved with a support ministry through their local church. The people involved in the ministry are with John and Sarah before, during, and after her passing. The ministry helps John finds peace and comfort during his time of sorrow, in which he is grateful.

Example # 2 involves Janice and her husband, Steve. Janice learns that Steve, like Sarah in example #1, has terminal cancer. Janice has never been very religious and does not regularly attend church. Stricken with grief over Steve's passing, Janice seeks counseling and support for widows. She finds a support group at a local church and begins to attend meetings. Janice finds the meetings to be of great help and becomes involved in the group, then begins attending worship services at the church.

Finally we have example # 3. Cory is a young man with a promising future. He was recently engaged to his girlfriend, Stephanie, and had just started a new job working in the technology field. Both of them came from Christian families and professed to have a belief in God. Just three weeks before their wedding, Stephanie was killed in a head-on collision with a drunk driver who also died in the crash. Cory was devastated. Not understanding how a loving and all-powerful God could let something like this happen, Cory expresses his anger with God and withdraws from religion.

Three different examples of how different people experience the death of a loved one. I used these examples specifically because they are real. Although I changed their names, the people mentioned here are actual people that I interacted with. Each person's experience had an equally important impact on their faith. Undoubtedly, each of these people have a slightly different relationship with God based on what they personally experienced. This is how the tiny variations of one's faith are shaped.

I have long rejected the notion that God 'robo-stamped' our faith. The idea that our beliefs rolled off an assembly line, identical to all others, devalues religion in just about every way possible. It is possible to share different beliefs about Christianity while also being obedient to God. I, myself, am quite different. Very few people who've known me long would consider me to be their image of a faith leader. I have tattoos. I enjoy rock music, especially the hard stuff. For many years I smoked cigarettes, chewed tobacco, and drank liquor that was harder than the rock music I usually had playing. But none of these things kept me from receiving God's grace and answering a call to ministry. I gave up the unhealthy stuff and softened my image a bit (I've noticed this to be a trend each year as I get older). Even if I hadn't, I know now that God would still love me.

I wrote this book for two main reasons. First, I wanted to share my work, research, and witness with as many people as possible. My congregations get to hear me preach and banter on topics such as these each week. But why stop there? This book is a vehicle to share these works with people beyond the walls of the church. The second (and most personal) reason is that I wanted to preserve a small, important part of me for my kids, and their kids. I wanted them to know that there was more to my life than a tortured adolescence and writing tickets to speeding motorists. I wanted them to know that even though I endured so many bad things in my life and witnessed many horrors in my career, God was always there.

For these reasons I have brought this book to fruition. These lessons are taken from my sermon manuscripts just the way God spoke them to my heart. While I expect that many readers will have different beliefs than those of a Methodist policeman, I hope that you find them useful—or at least interesting.

David Clark was a middle-aged widow from a suburban New England neighborhood. He lived in a modest two-story home with a teenage son and eleven year old daughter. David lost his wife, Gina, to bone cancer two years ago. Despite the great tragedy he and his kids had endured, David zeroed his focus to parenting. After all, David had to earn the income of two parents while raising the children by himself. David stopped going to O'Malley's Pub to meet the guys on Monday and Thursday nights. Andy and Mike, David's best friends since childhood, hadn't seen or heard from him in over a year. David stopped going to the gym when Gina got sick. He wanted to spend as much time with his family as he could while he still had the chance. But after she passed, he decided that making sure the kids were taken care of was more important than exercise. With the exception of the kids, it seemed that David had given up the things in his life that made him 'David.' He was polite, well-liked by his co-workers, and he was a great dad. But David had become empty, and everyone could see it. He'd grown weary of people's half-hearted smiles when they passed him in the hallway at work and asked, "How are you holding up? How are things at home?" He just didn't have it in him anymore. He didn't even know what 'it' was, but it seemed that whatever it was had been buried along with Gina. One evening, David walks through the back door into the kitchen and set his briefcase and laptop on the floor next to the breakfast nook, which he'd done religiously for the past seventeen years. Then he noticed Katie and Jonathan sitting at the table silently, staring at him as if they had some sort of important news to tell him.

Katie says, "Sit down, dad. We need to talk."

Easing into his chair, David looks at both of them and says, "Ok, what's up, guys?"

"Dad, we appreciate all you do for us, but you're not you anymore. You don't do anything for yourself. We miss you, we miss who you used to be before mom died."

Stunned, David managed to reply, "I'm still me. I just have to focus on taking care of you two. I don't have time to waste on anything else."

"Dad, we're good. We can manage. We want you to be happy. We talked about it and we think you should start dating again. It's ok."

Somewhat irritated, David got up and headed toward the living room, mumbling, "I'm fine, I don't need to date anyone."

About half an hour passed, David sat on the edge of his bed. "It's Wednesday night. The church is open. Gina used to always drag me along to Bible study. I miss that….God, give me strength! I miss her so much! The kids are right, I don't even know who I am anymore! God, help me, guide me! Show me who I'm supposed to be now!"

An hour later David pulls into the parking lot at Saint Stephen's Church. As he walked down the hallway of the Family Life Center toward the classrooms where they held bible studies, he hears a raspy, gruff voice, "David Clark! Good to see you again!"

He turned and saw Jerry, an older man from the church who'd led some one of the classes that he had attended with Gina. Jerry was a friendly guy. He loved talking about sports and cars, and of course the Bible. Jerry came to the hospital when both of the kids were born.

"Hey, Jerry," David said, pleased to see a familiar face.

"David, I want you to meet my niece, Samantha. I think you two would have a lot to talk about, she's a cancer survivor."

Before David could decline, Jerry motioned to someone inside the classroom and a beautiful, young woman with long blonde hair and an amazing smile walked out and extended her hand.

"David, hi! I'm so glad to finally meet you! My uncle has told me a lot about you!"

This story sounds like the plot to a Hallmark movie that suggests an ending with hope and joy. It's not a true story, just something I made up. As the author I have created a sense of sadness in David. I've made David's children a bit more mature about the situation they are in. I created lovable Jerry, the old guy that all of us want to see at church. And then I created Samantha, the human embodiment of hope and joy for our melancholy David. No matter how much I market this, or any other story, as fiction, there will always be some truth, some factual part me in this story as the author.

We, too, are the main characters in the stories of our lives. God is our author, and every author inlays a part of themselves into their work. For us, that means our Divine Author, God, is hope and joy to look forward to in our lives.

Romans 15:4-13:

15:4 For whatever was written in former days was written for our instruction, so that by steadfastness and by the encouragement of the scriptures we might have hope. 5 May the God of steadfastness and encouragement grant you to live in harmony with one another, in accordance with Christ Jesus, 6 so that together you may with one voice glorify the God and Father of our Lord Jesus Christ.

7 Welcome one another, therefore, just as Christ has welcomed you, for the glory of God. 8 For I tell you that Christ has become a servant of the circumcised on behalf of the truth of God in order that he might confirm the promises given to the patriarchs, 9 and in order that the Gentiles might glorify God for his mercy. As it is written,

"Therefore I will confess you among the Gentiles,

  and sing praises to your name";

10 and again he says,

"Rejoice, O Gentiles, with his people";

11 and again,

"Praise the Lord, all you Gentiles,

  and let all the peoples praise him";

12 and again Isaiah says,

"The root of Jesse shall come,

  the one who rises to rule the Gentiles;

in him the Gentiles shall hope."

13 May the God of hope fill you with all joy and peace in believing, so that you may abound in hope by the power of the Holy Spirit.

In these weeks just before the Christmas season, we celebrate knowing that there is more to come. Our story isn't finished. Like with David and Samantha, we can anticipate hope and joy. It's not about Christmas trees and wrapping paper and hot apple cider. It's the celebration of one more chapter of our story completed, with more to come. The story of our lives is not yet finished. The story of Jesus Christ on Earth is not yet finished. The story of God is not yet finished. We have not yet seen the end. And because of that we have hope, we have joy.

"Hail to the King"

C hrist the King: what does this divine title really mean? What is Christ the King of? Jews? All of humanity? Pontius Pilate asked this very question after Jesus was arrested.

John 18:33-37:

18:33 Then Pilate entered the headquarters again, summoned Jesus, and asked him, "Are you the King of the Jews?" 34 Jesus answered, "Do you ask this on your own, or did others tell you about me?" 35 Pilate replied, "I am not a Jew, am I? Your own nation and the chief priests have handed you over to me. What have you done?" 36 Jesus answered, "My kingdom is not from this world. If my kingdom were from this world, my followers would be fighting to keep me from being handed over to the Jews. But as it is, my kingdom is not from here." 37 Pilate asked him, "So you are a king?" Jesus answered, "You say that I am a king. For this I was born, and for this I came into the world, to testify to the truth. Everyone who belongs to the truth listens to my voice."

The Passion of the Christ: the most significant story ever told in history. This excerpt of the story clarifies Jesus' authority. Pilate asks Jesus, "Are you a king?" The interesting thing here is that Jesus never directly claims the title of "King." He makes reference to 'His kingdom' being 'not from this world.' He says, "...my kingdom is not far from here." But He never calls Himself a king. Nor does He deny it.

So what is a king? Well, in Jesus' time the kings of Israel and Judah were believed to be God's agents, chosen to rule their respective nations. Their monarchy was established by the Scriptures of the Old Testament. While these kings were granted vast power they demanded allegiance from their people. The king, however, did not serve his people. The king served God. The king's allegiance was to Yahweh...to Hashem. The king was not in charge of the judicial system. This was left up to the chief priests and if a person violated the law, they were punished according to Scripture. The king was not always a well-liked person. The king would often have to draft men for military service against their will. 1 Samuel indicates that the king had the right to take men for military service, women for domestic service, land and part of a person's harvest, flocks and herds of livestock, and could require state service in support of the monarchy from any person or animal. Obviously, these things wouldn't have been all that popular.

Jesus wasn't a king like that though. Jesus' kingdom isn't confined to land inside the borders of a nation. Jesus' kingdom does not require drafting men for military service, or women for servanthood. The treasury is not filled with gold and jewels. No! The kingdom that Jesus speaks of has a treasury filled with grace...with God's love...with eternal life. The walls of this kingdom are not built with bricks and mortar. The walls of this kingdom are built with faith. The gates of this kingdom are not heavily guarded, anyone can come into this glorious kingdom. Citizenship is easy.

In verse 37 Jesus tells us how to become citizens in His kingdom, saying, "Everyone who belongs to the truth listens to my voice." If you want to become a loyal subject in this kingdom all you have to do is hear the truth and believe.

But Jesus does have one thing in common with the other kings: He asks for your complete allegiance. Complete allegiance to Christ the King means that we bow down to His authority no matter what the situation is. It means we completely trust in Him, even through the storms in our lives. It means we willingly accept His grace, and give thanks for it.

If anyone says to us, "You must abandon your beliefs because they offend me, there is no God at all," we shall reply, "No! For I am a servant of Jesus Christ, the King of Kings, and there is no other way to get where I'm going except through Him. Let me tell you about my King..."

Some kings live in grand palaces where we're not permitted to go. Christ the King lives in my modest home with me.

Some kings charge a tax on his people. Christ the King gives everything to us freely.

Some kings will never know the names of most of the servants in their kingdoms. Christ the King knows the hearts of everyone who serves Him.

Some kings keep vast treasures. Christ the King treasures us above all else.

We profess our allegiance to Christ the King. There will be no doubt of whom we serve. I have heard the truth. I have heard the voice of the Lord. I am a servant in the Kingdom of God. I serve the King of Kings. Christ the King. Hail to the King!

I used to do a lot of bicycling in my youth when my knees were still good. My friend, Mike, and I would spend hours riding up and down the county roads on our "ten-speeds" until the sun started to go down. That's when we knew it was time to go back home. I remember the first time we rode all the way into town, which was about five miles from our neighborhood. We thought we were big shots going all that way on our own down the highway. The one thing that stands out in my memory the most about that day was my exhaustion having to pedal up several big hills. I recall getting about half way up the second hill, which was a gradual incline of about a half a mile, and I had to stop. My leg muscles burned. And poor Mike, he was a chubby kid, he started panting just from looking at the hill. We both accepted our shame of defeat as we walked our bikes up to the top. Then, going downhill was really fast and we barely even had to pedal. That was the fun part. We continued this routine, ride down one side of the big hills, walk up to the top of the next one. By the time we got to town, we were too tired to do much and we had burned a good part of the daylight. I thought to myself, "Wouldn't it be great if the whole trip was somehow all downhill? I wouldn't be so tired and it wouldn't take so long to get here."

Friends, Jesus Christ is standing at the top of the hill right now. And He wants us to take out all the stops and make a straight path right to us.

Luke 3:2-6.

3:2...the word of God came to John son of Zechariah in the wilderness. 3 He went into all the region around the

Jordan, proclaiming a baptism of repentance for the forgiveness of sins, 4 as it is written in the book of the words of the prophet Isaiah,

"The voice of one crying out in the wilderness:

'Prepare the way of the Lord,

make his paths straight.

5 Every valley shall be filled,

and every mountain and hill shall be made low,

and the crooked shall be made straight,

and the rough ways made smooth;

6 and all flesh shall see the salvation of God.'"

So our scripture is telling us several different things. Here we have John the Baptist who is led to proclaim that we must prepare for the coming of the Messiah. He goes on to quote Isaiah who, by the way, is the most quoted prophet in the New Testament. And in this quote Isaiah tells us to prepare this divine path for the Lord; it should be a straight-shot, all the valleys filled in, mountains leveled out. Just a straight path straight to us, and we will see it in the form of our salvation. John the Baptist doesn't just quote Isaiah, but he also tells us how we prepare this path. And we do that by a baptism of repentance.

Baptism of repentance: let's examine what that means. The word "baptism" comes from the Greek transliteration of "*baptizo*," meaning to immerse. While the early Christian church was the first to use the word "baptism" it is not the first to practice the ritual. No, contrary to popular belief, baptisms were not started by John the Baptist. John the Baptist was actually practicing a Jewish

20

ritual called *"tevilah,"* which was a ritual washing of the body by immersion in a *'mikveh.'* This ritual was used to restore a person's condition to a state of purity.

John the Baptist was likely among the first, however, to refer to this ritual as a sacrament, and it was one of the only two sacraments taken by Jesus Himself. But John the Baptist's meaning of the ritual was a good bit different from the Jewish custom, which only restored an unclean person to a state of holy purity. The details of when a person practiced this Jewish ritual are fairly disgusting, but let's just say that they cleanse their bodies in a very literal sense. John the Baptist was led by to begin baptizing people on a deeper level, a manner in which the Holy Spirit, not the water, cleansed the filth of the soul, rather than the flesh. For the person being baptized, it's a powerful moment in their life where they make an outward profession of an inward faith, publicly showing their devotion to God, acknowledging their sin, and repenting it. In the United Methodist Church we baptize by sprinkling, pouring, and immersion. We do not re-baptize people, God got it right the first time.

And now I'll start a debate. Listen closely, friends: a water baptism is not required for entry into Heaven. Nor is it sufficient for salvation. As Christ hangs from the cross, two condemned thieves named Gestas and Dismas are crucified next to Him. Gestas gives Jesus a hard time, mocking Him about the being the Messiah. Dismas, known to history as the 'penitent thief' defends Jesus and asks for mercy. Jesus tells Dismas in Luke 23:43, "Truly I tell you, today you will be with me in Paradise." Why is this? Because baptism has very little to do with water and everything to do with immersing ourselves in the Holy Spirit. Dismas repented, and that's what baptism is all about: Baptism of repentance.

Repentance is the key, and it's necessary in every stage of Christian life. Repentance makes straight the Lord's path to us. Repentance clears the obstacles, and once all the things that stand between us and the Lord, have been done away with, do you know what happens? All flesh shall see the salvation of God.

The season of Advent is a season of preparation. We prepare for Christ's arrival, we prepare to share the Good News, but most of all we prepare ourselves, in heart, mind, and soul

A s we begin the season of Advent, I'm reminded that
God gives us signs. These signs guide us through
the day, through the seasons, through our life, even
through the generations. Think about all the signs God gives
us. The birds flying south are a sign that winter is coming.
Dark clouds forming in the distance are a sign that rain is
coming. Think about all the signs that our bodies give us (I
know when my stomach starts growling it means I'm about
to eat). There are so many signs in our lives we could spend
the whole sermon segment listing them.

Signs are forecasts of things to come. Meteorologists
have made an art of forecasting the weather. This task is
probably a little more difficult for meteorologists in Texas
with our unpredictable weather, but forecasting weather
means looking for signs, and looking for these signs means
paying attention to details. Now, for some reason or another
I actually took a meteorology class years ago. Modern
weatherpersons have all kinds of expensive technology to
help them gather up details barometric pressure,
temperatures, moisture content in the air, all kinds of things
that help them make a prediction about the weather. But
before all this technology and weather reports, we had to
make the forecasts the old fashioned way. When there was
a high moisture content in the air, pine cones will close up
before it rains. Dandelions close each night. If you see one
that doesn't open in the morning, there's rain a' coming. In
this hemisphere of North America, most storms move west
to northeast. When the wind blows from the east, hang on,
because that indicates a low-pressure system is moving in

with strong storms. It's the small details like the dandelion and the wind blowing that help us make a prediction. While we often joke about the accuracy of the local news channel's forecasts, this art is actually extremely important. We prepare for whatever the forecast is. And these preparations make huge differences. Perhaps it results in moving an outdoor wedding somewhere indoors. Or delaying an airplane from taking off and landing. It could even mean the difference between life and death in the event of severe weather, or extreme temperatures.

The details in our text do, in fact, make the difference between life and death; or rather death and eternal life.

Luke 21:25-36:

21:25 "There will be signs in the sun, the moon, and the stars, and on the earth distress among nations confused by the roaring of the sea and the waves. 26 People will faint from fear and foreboding of what is coming upon the world, for the powers of the heavens will be shaken. 27 Then they will see 'the Son of Man coming in a cloud' with power and great glory. 28 Now when these things begin to take place, stand up and raise your heads, because your redemption is drawing near."

29 Then he told them a parable: "Look at the fig tree and all the trees; 30 as soon as they sprout leaves you can see for yourselves and know that summer is already near. 31 So also, when you see these things taking place, you know that the kingdom of God is near. 32 Truly I tell you, this generation will not pass away until all things have taken place. 33 Heaven and earth will pass away, but my words will not pass away.

34 "Be on guard so that your hearts are not weighed down with dissipation and drunkenness and the worries of this life, and that day does not catch you unexpectedly, 35 like a trap. For it will come upon all who live on the face of the whole earth. 36 Be alert at all times, praying that you may have the strength to escape all these things that will take place, and to stand before the Son of Man."

In this text Jesus elaborates on the things to come that he foretold in our previous texts over the past few weeks. While these events seem like a grim warning, Jesus is telling the disciples of signs that are meant to give them hope.

He's telling them that "although things will be hard, although life will be scary, God's glory is just around the corner!" He goes on to warn them not to let the difficult times lead them to squandering their lives and giving in to sin. Be ready, God's glory is just around the corner!

The Advent is a time to look for signs, a time to prepare ourselves for the coming of Our Savior. This is the beginning of a new Christian year. New beginnings, a new lease on our own spiritual lives, a new mission for the church. Our past is behind us, everything that happened yesterday and the day before. We've had some successes, we've had some failures, and now we prepare ourselves again to surrender our lives to Christ.

What signs are you seeing in your life? What signs do you see during this holiday season of God's goodness and grace? For every sign you can identify, realize that it is a forecast of greater things to come.

"Now What?"

D o you profess to be one of Christ's disciples? If so, that's great! Professing our faith regularly is a good thing! Ok, now what should we do? That is the question posed in our Scripture for this lesson. Here it is, the season of Advent, symbolizing our preparation of the arrival of Jesus Christ. We know the basics of what Jesus taught us, what we should do and not do. So what else? Is that it? How do we be Christians? We pick up where John the Baptist delivers his first "sermon."

Luke 3:7-17:

3:7 John said to the crowds that came out to be baptized by him, "You brood of vipers! Who warned you to flee from the wrath to come? 8 Bear fruits worthy of repentance. Do not begin to say to yourselves, 'We have Abraham as our ancestor'; for I tell you, God is able from these stones to raise up children to Abraham. 9 Even now the ax is lying at the root of the trees; every tree therefore that does not bear good fruit is cut down and thrown into the fire."

10 And the crowds asked him, "What then should we do?" 11 In reply he said to them, "Whoever has two coats must share with anyone who has none; and whoever has food must do likewise." 12 Even tax collectors came to be baptized, and they asked him, "Teacher, what should we do?" 13 He said to them, "Collect no more than the amount prescribed for you." 14 Soldiers also asked him, "And we, what should we do?" He said to them, "Do not extort money from anyone by threats or false accusation, and be satisfied with your wages."

15 As the people were filled with expectation, and all were questioning in their hearts concerning John, whether he might be the Messiah, 16 John answered all of them by saying, "I baptize you with water; but one who is more powerful than I is coming; I am not worthy to untie the thong of his sandals. He will baptize you with the Holy Spirit and fire. 17 His winnowing fork is in his hand, to clear his threshing floor and to gather the wheat into his granary; but the chaff he will burn with unquenchable fire."

So John admonishes this crowd of people who've come to be baptized. He warns them that they have to repent and they're like, "Ok...so now what?" What's interesting is that John's answers all concern the use and desire for money, insinuating that one's true priorities can be revealed by cancelled checks.

So I'm a Christian, I've been baptized, I've professed my faith in Christ. What do I do now?

A lot of folks think that being a Christian means living a Christian lifestyle. Well, friends, that's only half of it. We also have to breathe it. What do I mean by that? Well, think about this in medical terms: can you live if you only inhale and never exhale? Can you live if you only exhale and never inhale?

The same is true for discipleship. We must inhale the Holy Spirit, and exhale the Holy Spirit. When we go to church, pray, hear the Gospel, follow the rules, we are inhaling the Spirit. When we exhale we are sharing our spiritual gifts with others. We exhale joy. We exhale God's love. We exhale the fruits of the Spirit. The mission of the church of is to make disciples of Christ for the transformation of the world. How do we make disciples? By exhaling the Holy Spirit.

When I meet someone for the first time and they say to me, "I'm a Christian," I think to myself, "Hmmm." I don't care what they look like, or how they're dressed, or any of that. I'm not judging them, but I *am* looking for signs that they are, in fact, a Christian. You see, professing faith means very little if there are no fruits of the Spirit to back it up.

So, I had someone once tell me, "I'm a Christian, but I don't go to church. I can pray to God just as well from the golf course as I can in the sanctuary." Have you ever heard someone say this? Friends, I'm tired of the lie! What a load of manure! You don't go to the golf course to pray, just like you don't go church to putt! Words are meaningless without action.

The hardest thing about making disciples is getting people to come to church. So, here's what we do: Go preach the gospel everywhere you can to whomever you can, but only use words as a last resort. You see, by living the gospel, by sharing our spiritual gifts, exhaling the Spirit, we make disciples. Acts of kindness like the Angel Tree program are exhaling the Spirit. Praying over strangers is exhaling the Spirit. Feed the hungry. Give money to the poor. Care for the sick and elderly. Help the oppressed and those who have suffered injustice. Shelter the homeless. Share the joy. Exhale the Spirit. And when you exhale the Spirit, you tell others you're a Christian without saying a word. That's what makes disciples.

You're a Christian. What do you do now?

ometimes life gets us down. Sometimes we perceive that we are but lowly, insignificant beings in the grand scheme of God's Creation. Some of us are poor. Some of us are sick and feeble. Some of us are nearing the end of our mortal lives and feel useless. Some of us are grieving the loss of loved ones. Some of us are just plain tired, looking for rest.

Friends, it's time for some Good News for a change! The angel, Gabriel, has visited Zechariah and Elizabeth (who was believed to be a distant cousin of Mary) and foretold the birth of John the Baptist. Six months after that Gabriel appears to Mary and Joseph and foretells of the birth of Jesus. An event known as the Annunciation. And not only that, Gabriel tells Mary that she will be the mother of the Son of God. No pressure, right? Gabriel goes on to tell Mary of Elizabeth's pregnancy and Mary goes to visit her.

Luke 1:39-55:

1:39 In those days Mary set out and went with haste to a Judean town in the hill country, 40 where she entered the house of Zechariah and greeted Elizabeth. 41 When Elizabeth heard Mary's greeting, the child leaped in her womb. And Elizabeth was filled with the Holy Spirit 42 and exclaimed with a loud cry, "Blessed are you among women, and blessed is the fruit of your womb. 43 And why has this happened to me, that the mother of my Lord comes to me? 44 For as soon as I heard the sound of your greeting, the child in my womb leaped for joy. 45 And blessed is she who believed that there would be a fulfillment of what was spoken to her by the Lord."

46 And Mary said,

"My soul magnifies the Lord,

47   and my spirit rejoices in God my Savior,

48 for he has looked with favor on the lowliness of his servant.

Surely, from now on all generations will call me blessed;

49 for the Mighty One has done great things for me,

and holy is his name.

50 His mercy is for those who fear him

from generation to generation.

51 He has shown strength with his arm;

he has scattered the proud in the thoughts of their hearts.

52 He has brought down the powerful from their thrones,

and lifted up the lowly;

53 he has filled the hungry with good things,

and sent the rich away empty.

54 He has helped his servant Israel,

in remembrance of his mercy,

55 according to the promise he made to our ancestors,

to Abraham and to his descendants forever."

If you ever feel lowly, remember this passage. Here you have two women who, in that time, were considered to be property more than they were anything else. Women of that day were only regarded as slightly a step up from the servants. In that culture, women just weren't all that significant. On top of that, you have Elizabeth, who was barren and in her old age; an elderly woman. And then there's Mary, a woman from Nazareth. Nazareth is not a large community. The population is estimated to be somewhere between 150 to 300 people. It is a relatively poor area at the time. And of all the people in the world Mary is the chosen to be the mother of our Lord.

Hidden within the lines of our text is the true message of Christmas. Christmas gives us hope. Children who live in poverty and are used to going without, often receive wonderful presents. The lonely get visitors they normally don't have. People doing kind things for one another are demonstrating God's love for us. You see, in some ways all of us are a poverty-stricken child, or a lonely shut-in, or feeble elderly person. We all have something that causes us to hope for more. Just as Elizabeth, who was elderly and barren, would conceive John the Baptist. Because of God's love, grace, and blessing, she would fulfill her dreams of motherhood. And Mary, a commoner from a small, poor community would bear the Christ Child. As Mary quotes in our Scripture today, "...for he has looked with favor on the lowliness of his servant."

This is the Good News to come. We don't have to be rich, or famous, or powerful, or all-righteous. We can be the broken, stressed out, financially-strapped servants of God that we are and God will still bless us. New birth, new life, new things are ahead, right around the corner.

"What Are You Afraid Of?"

Matthew 2:1-12

2:1 In the time of King Herod, after Jesus was born in Bethlehem of Judea, wise men from the East came to Jerusalem, 2 asking, "Where is the child who has been born king of the Jews? For we observed his star at its rising, and have come to pay him homage." 3 When King Herod heard this, he was frightened, and all Jerusalem with him; 4 and calling together all the chief priests and scribes of the people, he inquired of them where the Messiah was to be born. 5 They told him, "In Bethlehem of Judea; for so it has been written by the prophet:

6 'And you, Bethlehem, in the land of Judah,

are by no means least among the rulers of Judah;

for from you shall come a ruler

who is to shepherd my people Israel.'"

7 Then Herod secretly called for the wise men and learned from them the exact time when the star had appeared. 8 Then he sent them to Bethlehem, saying, "Go and search diligently for the child; and when you have found him, bring me word so that I may also go and pay him homage." 9 When they had heard the king, they set out; and there, ahead of them, went the star that they had seen at its rising, until it stopped over the place where the child was. 10 When they saw that the star had stopped, they were overwhelmed with joy. 11 On entering the house, they saw the child with Mary his mother; and they knelt down and paid him homage. Then, opening their treasure chests, they offered him gifts of gold, frankincense, and myrrh. 12 And having been warned in a dream not to return to Herod, they left for their own country by another road.

As human beings we are naturally hardwired for certain survival instincts. One of these instincts is our reaction to fear. For some unknown reason, we seemingly put reason and logic to the back-burner when we feel threatened, even when there is little actual threat. Take bugs for example. Are you afraid of bugs? I know certain people who will scream and jump out of a moving car at 70 miles per hour when they notice a tiny, harmless bug crawling on them. Friends, this is not rational. Especially if the bug does not sting or bite or carry any diseases. A bug weighs a few milligrams, a human weighs substantially more. Bugs aren't generally very smart. Humans are. When a bug is crawling on our leg it doesn't typically seem to be aware that it's in danger of being squished. We're bigger, smarter, and have the tactical element of surprise in the war on bugs. So why is it that so many people have such an unreasonable fear of them? I've literally seen people stop what they're doing, take precious time out of their lives and spend big money on pesticides because they had to kill a spider in the driveway. Why? Because we fear what *could be*.

Snakes are another critter that often cause people to lose their sense of reason. I've heard plenty of people say, "The only good snake is a dead snake." While there are some dangerous snakes out there, any farmer or biologist will tell you that snakes are an important part of our ecosystem and are beneficial to agriculture. Snakes consume more rodents than almost any other animal. This keeps the rodent population down, reducing damage to crops and having to use chemical means to control them.

Additionally, there are a number of harmless snakes that eat poisonous snakes. Despite all this, a good majority of people are seriously afraid of snakes.

Herod had a similar fear of Christ. Scripture gives us no specific reason for Herod's fear, but his reaction was certainly irrational. It is widely speculated that Herod's fear was due to politics. Herod was an agent of Rome. Herod served a government that sought to oppress Jewish influence. Because of Jesus' widely publicized arrival and the rumors that had spread across the land that he was the Messiah, Herod most likely saw this as a threat to his control over Judea. He sends out the wise men, the Magi, to locate Jesus and report back. Fortunately, the Magi do not share the same fear as Herod, and they keep Christ's location a secret in order to protect him.

Herod's fear was not rational, and because of this he missed the greatest opportunity of his life. While having the endorsement of a Roman Emperor certainly gave him power, imagine if he had God's endorsement. Instead Herod's actions would drive the Holy Family to seek refuge in Egypt and result in the death of many innocent children.

While our irrational thoughts and feelings don't generally go this far, we need to stop and ask ourselves, "Am I really thinking this through? Are my actions reasonable?" Friends, God leads us to challenges, people, situations, all kinds of things, affording us grace to make decisions of our own will. And in making decisions we have to be rational. I remember when I was a police chief sitting on an interview board with several other city officials. We were selecting candidates for openings in the department. We'd interviewed several applicants and came down to our final selections. One applicant had a college degree and police experience. Despite his lack of experience, some of the interview board immediately voiced their preference because of his degree. The second applicant had several years of experience in law enforcement. One of the members of the interview board stated that he had heard something bad about the man from someone else in the community. However, I had received good reports from his last employers. I decided to hire both of the applicants. The man with the college degree turned out to be a terrible police officer and resigned several months later to pursue what came to be a lucrative real estate career. The older man with experience who had not been favored by the interview board turned out to be an outstanding officer and continues to serve the law enforcement community to this day. Had we decided to listen to the rumors of "what could be true" we would have missed out on a good employee, and his life would have certainly taken a different course if we had not given him a chance.

Are our fears and reactions based on sense and reason? Or are we acting irrationally? How does God factor into the equation of our decision making process? Grace is a funny thing. Sometimes we're the leg, sometimes we're the bug.

"Life Insurance"

Getting my high school diploma wasn't the easiest thing in the world for me. Academically I was able to make good grades. I breezed through elementary school. Middle school was a little tougher, but I was still in good shape grade-wise. History class, sports, and playing drums in the band were my favorite things. Then I got to high school and I struggled to maintain the honors classes I was in, not because of grades but because of my attitude. I didn't enjoy studies on Dante's Inferno and the Canterbury Tales. Writing reports about the works of Burke and Milton wore me out. Algebra was my least favorite of all things. I'd rather crawl on my hands and knees through five miles of broken glass than solve a matrix. I rejected the idea that I needed to know these things. My only focus at that time was to get out of school so I could go to Marine Corps boot camp. At some point I finally had the epiphany: "If I want to graduate from high school and go the Marines, I have to pass all these classes." In addition to my full school day, I ended up picking up extra credits in night school and taking correspondence classes. After I finally accepted what had to be in order to graduate, my graduation was realized. A year early even.

Baptism works kind of the same way. Once we accept the word of God as our rule and guide, and accept Christ as our Savior, we mark the beginning of the rest of our lives with a ceremony of sorts. As United Methodists we describe baptism as an outward profession of an inward faith, meaning we're showing our acceptance of Christ into our lives. And as Methodists we only baptize once. But if that was all there was to baptism, this would be a really short sermon. So now I tell you there is more than only one form of baptism in our Christian lives.

Acts 8:14-17:

8:14 Now when the apostles at Jerusalem heard that Samaria had accepted the word of God, they sent Peter and John to them. 15 The two went down and prayed for them that they might receive the Holy Spirit 16 (for as yet the Spirit had not come upon any of them; they had only been baptized in the name of the Lord Jesus). 17 Then Peter and John laid their hands on them, and they received the Holy Spirit.

I remember as kid being asked if I had been baptized. Some of my friends from other denominations would tell me I had to be sure, that my salvation was directly linked to my baptism, and that if I wasn't old enough to understand it, then it didn't count. Some of them even said that if I died right then, I would go to Hell. Of course this terrified me and I felt ridiculed by these people. But they were just expressing what they thought they'd been taught out concern for me. Let's ponder that question: "Have I been baptized?" We'll revisit that question in a minute.

I remember being called to the scene of a horrific car accident in which several people had died, including two children. I can recall one of the firemen standing next to me saying, "Well, I sure hope they were baptized." His statement not was not only appalling, it angered me especially since I had to deliver the news of their death to their parents. Where was the trust in God? Where was the mercy and grace? The statement sounded like baptism was part of a club membership. I went home and thought about that appalling statement. It became obvious to me that while different faith traditions regard baptism differently, we all regard baptism as the ultimate form of life insurance.

As many of you have heard me say before, for most people salvation is a process rather than an event. It takes time. Baptism is part of that process. Most often imagine a baptismal font or being dunked in a river when we think of being baptized. This is an outward profession of an inward faith. This is being baptized in the name of the Lord Jesus. I, and many pastors, will give you a certificate when we perform this sacrament. It is a pinpointed time, date, and location. But there's another form of baptism that occurs. In Luke 3:16 John the Baptist talks about baptizing people with water, but goes on to say that the Messiah "...will baptize you with the Holy Spirit and fire."

There you have it. Baptism also comes from Christ, not with water, but with the Holy Spirit. While denominations argue procedural matters of whether a person has to be repeatedly baptized to be a member of the church, or whether one has to be baptized by a preacher with water, John the Baptist lays it out there for us: Christ will baptize us with the Holy Spirit and fire.

What's the difference? When we decide to accept the practices of our church we are baptized by water. But when we accept the word of God, when we accept Christ Jesus as Savior of our lives, we are baptized by the Holy Spirit. And when Jesus baptizes us, He doesn't just baptize with the Holy Spirit, but with fire also. While that might sound like a bad thing, it's actually not. Water washes filth away, yes. But fire refers to the Pentecost. Fire purifies better than anything else. It destroys filth. When we see these wildfires on the news, we see the fire destroy all that's in its path. But what happens next? New trees and vegetation begin to grow. New animals move into the area. And that's the significance in this text. Our burden of sin is destroyed, taken away, and we are given new life.

I once went to a young man's house to arrest him for a couple arrest warrants. The warrants were for an assault he'd committed against his girlfriend. As I approached his front door, the man's mother came out on the porch. I told her who I was and why I was there, she told me that the man I was looking for was inside the house. She went inside and had the man come out and surrender to me.

He looked me in the face and said, "I have to be a man. God wants me to take responsibility for what I've done."

Granted, not all arrests happen this easily. But this guy had a valid point. We have to accept the reality of our sin. God wants us to do something about it. When we accept God's grace, when we accept the word of God, when we accept Christ as our Savior, we become baptized by the Holy Spirit. The certificate you receive for that baptism isn't written on paper. But it does become your life insurance policy.

"Lesson from a Cajun"

In the late 1980's a middle-aged woman named Laura drove several hours to a rural area to a remote part of southern Louisiana. She arrived at her destination and was greeted at the front porch of an unassuming Victorian-era house by an elderly woman named Doris Bergeron, whom she had never met before. She had been referred to Doris to help her with an embarrassing problem. Laura's hand had an outbreak of stubborn warts that were resistant to conventional treatments. They just wouldn't go away. Although it was a longshot, Doris became her last hope before having to have the warts surgically removed. After a couple minutes of small-talk on the front porch, Doris (who was a devout Catholic) made the sign of the cross, took Laura's hand in one of her own, and used her other hand to draw circles above the affected area. After making the circles she made the sign of the cross again, and as she's doing this she's mumbling some sort of prayer in French. When she finished she told Laura that within six weeks the warts would be gone. Just a week after meeting with Doris the warts shrunk, and within three weeks they were completely gone, and never returned. This might sound like witchcraft, but Doris was, in fact, what's called a *"traiteur"* (pronounced *tray-tur*). A traiteur is a Cajun faith-healer. Traiteurs are devoutly religious Christian people, typically Roman Catholic. By saying prayers and laying their hands on people, they claim to be able to cure a number illnesses and ailments, and have done so for hundreds of years.

The traiteurs are not the only faith healers. A *"powwaw"* is a type of faith healer in the Pennsylvania Dutch culture, usually a devout Catholic, Lutheran, or Quaker. Like the traiteur, the powwaw would pray to God, usually in German, while laying hands on the person they were healing. Another common factor for both the traiteur and the powwaw is that they both declare that the people they heal are done so by the Holy Spirit, and that the ability to do this is a gift from God. Now, I've never seen this done first hand, but I can certainly attest to the healing power of prayer as a gift.

1 Corinthians 12:1-11:

12:1 Now concerning spiritual gifts, brothers and sisters, I do not want you to be uninformed. 2 You know that when you were pagans, you were enticed and led astray to idols that could not speak. 3 Therefore I want you to understand that no one speaking by the Spirit of God ever says "Let Jesus be cursed!" and no one can say "Jesus is Lord" except by the Holy Spirit.

4 Now there are varieties of gifts, but the same Spirit; 5 and there are varieties of services, but the same Lord; 6 and there are varieties of activities, but it is the same God who activates all of them in everyone. 7 To each is given the manifestation of the Spirit for the common good. 8 To one is given through the Spirit the utterance of wisdom, and to another the utterance of knowledge according to the same Spirit, 9 to another faith by the same Spirit, to another gifts of healing by the one Spirit, 10 to another the working of miracles, to another prophecy, to another the discernment of spirits, to another various kinds of tongues, to another the interpretation of tongues. 11 All these are activated by one and the same Spirit, who allots to each one individually just as the Spirit chooses.

While most of us don't have the gift of healing, God does grant gifts to each of us. So what are your gifts? Some people, like my son, Mason, have the gift of musical ability. Some people have the gift of leadership. Some people are gifted listeners, while some are caregivers. Teachers have a gift. Mechanics and farmers have gifts. What are *your* spiritual gifts? How are we sharing those gifts? How do we even know if it's a spiritual gift? Well, for one, a spiritual gift is something that you need not charge a fee or commission for. A spiritual gift is something that reflects God's love for us. And, just as importantly, a spiritual gift does not exclude any human being. It is a gift from God, given to you to share with others.

Often times, as Christians, we become a bit selfish when it comes to the mission of the church and the things we're supposed to be doing as disciples. I'm not picking on anyone in particular, but here's an example: going on a mission trip to help repair homes in a disaster area, while staying in a four-star hotel. What message does that send, especially to those outside the church? As Christians, we have a hard enough time getting others to understand what discipleship is about. Do you have any idea how difficult it is to explain the concept of the Holy Trinity to someone who has never heard of it before? So it's understandable that they are skeptical about Christians when we tell them our scripture says that God blesses the poor while we enjoy the luxuries we have. The mission of the church: To make disciples of Jesus Christ for the transformation of the world. That is our mission. I don't really like the way that's worded, saying we "make" disciples as if they're made of Lego bricks or something. The truth is none of us can change the heart of a person into becoming a disciple. Not you, not me. Only God can do that.

Instead, I think a more accurate wording would be, "To *inspire* disciples in Jesus Christ by sharing God's love for the transformation of the world." One of the best ways we can inspire discipleship is through the sharing of our spiritual gifts, especially with those who are outside the church, as well as with each other. Jesus tells us that we are to love God with all our heart, soul, and mind...and to love our neighbors as we love ourselves. These are the greatest commandments.

"The Needy Ones"

I want you take just a moment and think about how many different people it takes to run an institution of any sort. Let's take a church for example: there's the pastor, of course, who leads the ministry, the lay leaders and speakers who help lead the church, the committees who set the budgets and care for the building, the song leader who leads songs, the accompanist who plays the music, the worship committee people who make the bulletins and set up the sanctuary, the treasurer and secretary, the nursery workers, the youth leaders, the communion servers, ushers, acolytes, Sunday school teachers, district superintendents, and a bishop who appoints the pastor. And that's actually the short list. The point is that any well-run institution, ministry or otherwise, takes multiple people who depend on each other.

1 Corinthians 12:12-31:

12:12 For just as the body is one and has many members, and all the members of the body, though many, are one body, so it is with Christ. 13 For in the one Spirit we were all baptized into one body—Jews or Greeks, slaves or free—and we were all made to drink of one Spirit.

14 Indeed, the body does not consist of one member but of many. 15 If the foot would say, "Because I am not a hand, I do not belong to the body," that would not make it any less a part of the body. 16 And if the ear would say, "Because I am not an eye, I do not belong to the body," that would not make it any less a part of the body. 17 If the whole body were an eye, where would the hearing be? If the whole body were hearing, where would the sense of smell be? 18 But as it is, God arranged the members in the body, each one of them, as he chose. 19 If all were a single member, where would the body be? 20 As it is, there are many members, yet one body. 21 The eye cannot say to the hand, "I have no need of you," nor again the head to the feet, "I have no need of you." 22 On the contrary, the members of the body that seem to be weaker are indispensable, 23 and those members of the body that we think less honorable we clothe with greater honor, and our less respectable members are treated with greater respect; 24 whereas our more respectable members do not need this. But God has so arranged the body, giving the greater honor to the inferior member, 25 that there may be no dissension within the body, but the members may have the same care for one another. 26 If one member suffers, all suffer together with it; if one member is honored, all rejoice together with it.

27 Now you are the body of Christ and individually members of it. 28 And God has appointed in the church first apostles, second prophets, third teachers; then deeds of power, then gifts of healing, forms of assistance, forms of leadership, various kinds of tongues. 29 Are all apostles? Are all prophets? Are all teachers? Do all work miracles? 30 Do all possess gifts of healing? Do all speak in tongues? Do all interpret? 31 But strive for the greater gifts. And I will show you a still more excellent way.

So I remember when I was fourteen or fifteen years old, my girlfriend at the time broke up with me. Of course, at that age it was the end of the world for about three days. But later in the week one of our mutual friends told me that she had broken up with me because she said I was too needy. Ahhhhh....booooo! Too needy? Are you kidding me? That reminds me of a helpless puppy whining day and night for food and attention. Ok, so I might have been a little needy.

Socially, we often consider being needy to be an unfavorable characteristic. We typically try to avoid being needy. But when it comes to God this is something that we need to embrace. God doesn't mind if we're needy. In fact, God likes when we're needy. Whether we like it or not, we have an interdependency on one another, as well as with God. Paul reminds us that it's something that we need to embrace. When we need a doctor, go to a doctor. When we need to learn, go to a teacher. When we need a friend, go to a friend. Likewise, when someone comes to us, whether it be in our professional capacity, as a friend, or as a church member, we must be ready to help fulfill those needs. Embrace it.

Let me ask you this: When do we need God? All the time, right? The truth is that we need God's help with everything we do. During each worship service I pose the question, "Where did we see Jesus this week, and where do we need to see Jesus?" While we like to be strong in many regards, we also need to acknowledge our dependence on God. We need to hand over our weaknesses, our worries, our struggles, even our victories. We need God's love, grace, guidance, wisdom, courage—we need these things. And just as we must acknowledge our need for God, look around you. We need one another. Perhaps for guidance, or prayers, or friendship. For our spiritual gifts. We're needy, and that's ok. We're supposed to be.

"A More Excellent Way"

1 Corinthians 13:1-13

13:1 If I speak in the tongues of mortals and of angels, but do not have love, I am a noisy gong or a clanging cymbal. 2 And if I have prophetic powers, and understand all mysteries and all knowledge, and if I have all faith, so as to remove mountains, but do not have love, I am nothing. 3 If I give away all my possessions, and if I hand over my body so that I may boast, but do not have love, I gain nothing.

4 Love is patient; love is kind; love is not envious or boastful or arrogant 5 or rude. It does not insist on its own way; it is not irritable or resentful; 6 it does not rejoice in wrongdoing, but rejoices in the truth. 7 It bears all things, believes all things, hopes all things, endures all things.

8 Love never ends. But as for prophecies, they will come to an end; as for tongues, they will cease; as for knowledge, it will come to an end. 9 For we know only in part, and we prophesy only in part; 10 but when the complete comes, the partial will come to an end. 11 When I was a child, I spoke like a child, I thought like a child, I reasoned like a child; when I became an adult, I put an end to childish ways. 12 For now we see in a mirror, dimly, but then we will see face to face. Now I know only in part; then I will know fully, even as I have been fully known. 13 And now faith, hope, and love abide, these three; and the greatest of these is love.

So our lesson here is that love is necessary for Christian life. Without love we are nothing. It's hard to imagine the world without love. Imagine poetry without love: "Roses are red. Violets are blue. Those are the color of flowers. The end." No passion. Our whole lives would be like badly written poems.

1 John 4:16 says, ***"God is love, and those who abide in love abide in God, and God abides in them."*** Paul points out that love lasts forever. Whereas everything else passes away, love remains. Therefore, it accompanies us to, and adorns us in, eternity. It prepares us for, and constitutes, heaven. While we often regard love as a basic human emotion, we ought to regard it as the sum of all that is *good*, both mortal and eternal.

Emotions such as happiness or fear only last a while. Love is something that we are willing to change our lives for, even sacrifice ourselves for. I've known a few veterans in my time. I never heard one of them ever say they enlisted in the military because they are merely happy with their country. Because of love, we're willing to marry a person, we're willing to make a major long-term decision to be with that person. And often as a result of that love, we procreate and have new people to love. Because of love, we willingly go to work every day to earn a living so we can take care of our families. In our last days we should hope to be surrounded by family and friends who love us. After we pass away from this mortal life, they will stop seeing us, they will stop talking with us, and they will not be able to touch us. But they will continue to love us, and we will continue to love them knowing that heaven is love. When all else fades away, love remains from generation to generation and transgresses even death.

Love is much more than an emotion. It is the greatest spiritual gift. Not everyone is easy to love. Not everyone deserves our love. Nor do we all deserve God's love. And that's why love is the queen of all graces—because God gives His grace and love freely anyway.

"Be Careful What You Wish For"

I hear people all the time saying they wish they had more money, or a bigger house, or a better job, etcetera. We set our hearts on material prosperity. Is it ok to work hard and prosper? Sure it is, in moderation. But too much of a good thing is often dangerous. In this lesson I want to look at why we should be cautious about what we wish for and how that affects discipleship.

Luke 5:1-11:

5:1 Once while Jesus was standing beside the lake of Gennesaret, and the crowd was pressing in on him to hear the word of God, 2 he saw two boats there at the shore of the lake; the fishermen had gone out of them and were washing their nets. 3 He got into one of the boats, the one belonging to Simon, and asked him to put out a little way from the shore. Then he sat down and taught the crowds from the boat. 4 When he had finished speaking, he said to Simon, "Put out into the deep water and let down your nets for a catch." 5 Simon answered, "Master, we have worked all night long but have caught nothing. Yet if you say so, I will let down the nets." 6 When they had done this, they caught so many fish that their nets were beginning to break. 7 So they signaled their partners in the other boat to come and help them. And they came and filled both boats, so that they began to sink. 8 But when Simon Peter saw it, he fell down at Jesus' knees, saying, "Go away from me, Lord, for I am a sinful man!" 9 For he and all who were with him were amazed at the catch of fish that they had taken; 10 and so also were James and John, sons of Zebedee, who were partners with Simon. Then Jesus said to Simon, "Do not be afraid; from now on you will be catching people." 11 When they had brought their boats to shore, they left everything and followed him.

Jesus is the guy you want to take fishing with you! Here you have Simon Peter who has a fishing operation. He was a small business owner in his day with two boats and crew. But lately the fishing hasn't been so good. They'd gone fishing the previous night and didn't catch a thing. And when your job is to catch fish, and you don't catch any fish, it's hard to make a living. So, Jesus comes along and there's this crowd of people crowding around him. Jesus sees these two boats on the shore, hops in one of them, and tells Peter they're going fishing.

Peter's not a disciple yet, but he had enough interest in Jesus to entertain the commands. Every fisherman's hope is to fill their boat with fish. Well, not so many that they get in trouble with the Game Warden. Jesus knew that Peter and his crew needed fish. And just as Peter needed fish, Jesus needed disciples. Jesus tells him to drop his nets, and the nets start to fill up with fish. In fact, they fill so much that they begin to tear. The fishing is good all the sudden! It's so good that Peter summons the other boat, and it drops its nets in the water, and those nets start to fill up. Oh yeah, the fishing is good! Just keep reeling them in! But how much is enough? Peter and his crew filled up the boats with so many fish that the boats begin to sink. This was an eye-opening moment for Peter.

How much is too much? I have a friend, James, who had decided to start his own trucking company years ago. James was not rich, so he saved up his money for a down-payment on a truck. James's first truck was an older 1978 Peterbilt. I remember how impressed I was when I first saw it; it was blue with lots of chrome. So James started taking loads from here to there and he was making some pretty good money. After a couple years James decided to double his money by adding a second truck to his operation. So he financed another rig and hired a driver. Now James is really banking. So he adds a third truck to his fleet and hires another driver. A couple years go by and now James has six trucks on the road. He has a full-blown trucking operation with a ton of overhead that he has to pay. In fact, there's so much money coming and so many expenses that James has to hire another driver to take his spot so he could sit in his home-office all day and manage the finances. It was around this time that James told me he missed driving.

He said, "Ash, I'm bringing in nearly $100,000 a month, but my monthly expenses after paying my drivers, fuel, insurance, and everything else come out to about $90,000 a month." I pointed out that he was still bringing in about $10,000 a month and that was pretty darn good. Greed has its way of teaching us lessons. If you remember back round the year 2007 or 2008, fuel prices sky-rocketed. His profits tanked and business slowed dramatically. He had to lay off some of his drivers, and without those on the road making money, his business folded. He filed for bankruptcy. He didn't know when enough was enough, and his boat sank.

How important is prosperity and success? How important are our vocations compared to our discipleship? Verse 11 of our text says they left everything and followed Jesus. *Everything.* Friends, if you're trying to fill your boat with profit, or achievements, or success, let today be the day that you leave all that behind and follow Christ. Let today be the day that you realize true wealth has nothing to do with money, or material things.

"Blessed Woes"

Luke 6:17-26

6:17 He came down with them and stood on a level place, with a great crowd of his disciples and a great multitude of people from all Judea, Jerusalem, and the coast of Tyre and Sidon. 18 They had come to hear him and to be healed of their diseases; and those who were troubled with unclean spirits were cured. 19 And all in the crowd were trying to touch him, for power came out from him and healed all of them.

20 Then he looked up at his disciples and said:

"Blessed are you who are poor, for yours is the kingdom of God.

21 "Blessed are you who are hungry now, for you will be filled.

"Blessed are you who weep now, for you will laugh.

22 "Blessed are you when people hate you, and when they exclude you, revile you, and defame you on account of the Son of Man. 23 Rejoice in that day and leap for joy, for surely your reward is great in heaven; for that is what their ancestors did to the prophets.

24 "But woe to you who are rich, for you have received your consolation.

25 "Woe to you who are full now, for you will be hungry.

"Woe to you who are laughing now, for you will mourn and weep.

26 "Woe to you when all speak well of you, for that is what their ancestors did to the false prophets.

This text sounds very similar to the beatitudes in the Gospel of Matthew, but they're not. Here Jesus lists four blessings and four woes. Throughout Luke's Gospel, Jesus is often found speaking counterintuitive and expected words. At the time it was a world where wealth and prosperity were presumed to indicate divine favor, but Jesus taught the opposite. The poor, the hungry, and the weeping are blessed along with the hated, reviled, defamed, and excluded. While on the other hand you have the rich and the full and the jovial who are subjected to woes. These blessings and woes that Jesus talks about outline this new, divine value system where the wealthy no longer exploit their privileges, but rather share their privileges with those who are less fortunate.

Prosperity can be a dangerous thing. Gaining too much of it can sink us. Using it for the wrong purposes can destroy us. Keeping it for ourselves can devour us. John Wesley describes it as a "sweet poison." Now I can be a tough critic, but I have to give credit where it's due. I can think of no more extreme example of sharing privilege than that of Houston Texans defensive end JJ Watt. What did JJ do? Well, to begin with he made millions of dollars playing football. In fact, his estimated net worth at the end of the 2018 season was more than $100 million dollars. JJ has a pretty good life. He can buy just about whatever he wants. But when Hurricane Harvey hit the Houston area, JJ jump-started a relief fund with some of his own money that grew to $41 million for storm victims. Pretty cool, right? But it doesn't stop there. Following the mass school shooting at Santa Fe High School, JJ paid for the funerals of the ten high school students who died, including a foreign exchange student from Pakistan. And guess what—that wasn't the end of it either. JJ also gave $10,000 of his own money to help the family of a fallen firefighter pay for the funeral in his home-state of Wisconsin.

Many people wake up in the morning and try to figure out how to obtain more money. With more money we can buy more things. We can hire people to do things for us instead of doing it ourselves. We think we can make ourselves more comfortable. That's the "sweet" part of the poison. The poison, and the reality, is that there is nothing particularly holy or divine about our pursuit of wealth. It consumes our time, it corrupts our motives and priorities, and it can even become a false idol if we're not careful. And money isn't the only form of prosperity and wealth. Some people have a lot of possessions, some have a lot of spare time, some have special talents or gifts.

So you're probably wondering if the preacher is going to say that you should tithe these over to the church. Sure! We'd love that! How much? I'd say start with ten percent. That would be great. And in case you didn't know, "tithe" isn't a verb. It's a noun meaning *tenth*. But tithing is only one way of using your prosperity to serve God. There are thousands of charities out there. Thousands of folks are going without food, going without a home, going without shoes. Millions of people need medical care because they don't have insurance and can't afford to pay. The possibilities are endless.

"How Do I Love?"

I'm mostly a lectionary preacher, which means that I write my sermons according to the Christian liturgical calendar. And as much as we all hate to hear it, it's that time of year again where the pastor makes us aware of some of our shortcomings when in relation to Christ's teachings (some preachers would have you hear that every Sunday). God commands us to do all kinds of things. Don't steal. That's pretty easy for most us. Don't kill people. Again, this hasn't been a big problem for this congregation. Remember the Sabbath. Hey, we're here aren't we? We're even pretty good about following God's instructions that are not in the Ten Commandments. We tithe. We give to the needy. We're even pretty good at that love thy neighbor thing. So why is it that Christians tend to "pump the brakes" when it comes to loving our enemies?

Luke 6:27-38:

6:27 "But I say to you that listen, Love your enemies, do good to those who hate you, 28 bless those who curse you, pray for those who abuse you. 29 If anyone strikes you on the cheek, offer the other also; and from anyone who takes away your coat do not withhold even your shirt. 30 Give to everyone who begs from you; and if anyone takes away your goods, do not ask for them again. 31 Do to others as you would have them do to you.

32 "If you love those who love you, what credit is that to you? For even sinners love those who love them. 33 If you do good to those who do good to you, what credit is that to you? For even sinners do the same. 34 If you lend to those from whom you hope to receive, what credit is that to you?

Even sinners lend to sinners, to receive as much again. 35 But love your enemies, do good, and lend, expecting nothing in return. Your reward will be great, and you will be children of the Most High; for he is kind to the ungrateful and the wicked. 36 Be merciful, just as your Father is merciful.

37 "Do not judge, and you will not be judged; do not condemn, and you will not be condemned. Forgive, and you will be forgiven; 38 give, and it will be given to you. A good measure, pressed down, shaken together, running over, will be put into your lap; for the measure you give will be the measure you get back."

"Love our enemies…"

Blah! Leaves a bad taste in our mouths, doesn't it? While many of you are thinking, "Eh, I've heard this sermon already. Preacher preached it last year, and the year before," I have to pose to you the question, "Why is that?"

I'll tell you why. It's because humanity as a whole has done a poorer job at following this commandment than just about any other. And I'm including myself in this statistic. It's important to know my strengths and weaknesses and be honest about them. I'm Scottish, Irish, and a quarter Italian—I can be as hot tempered as they come. Usually the last thing I want to do when someone makes me angry is love them.

So when I was taking psychology classes many moons ago, I learned one really effective method to identifying things about ourselves called 'emotional inference through word-association.' So I'm going to give you all some words and phrases, and I want you to think about how it makes you feel. Is something we associate as friendly, or something in the enemy category? So bear with me during this exercise...

Dog, mother, disciple, Democrat, family, Muslim, Christmas Tree, man, homosexual, child, conservative, gangster, teacher, bridesmaid, government, Chicago, George Strait, Viet Cong...

If I have made you more uncomfortable than you'd planned on, then I have done what I set out to do. I've mixed together a bunch of things that we don't generally associate together. Some of the things are things you like, and some of the things you likely consider to be a threat.

Do we love them all? Probably not. And that is why Christian preachers across the world are preach on this topic again and again. We've been brainwashed over the span of our lives that it's ok to reject and repel our perceived enemies—that it's ok to dish-out to them all of the Old Testament, and none of the Gospel. We often find ourselves led in our beliefs by people and policies that are not scripturally-based. We end up with enemies, for one reason or another. But as a pastor of the Christian-faith, I tell you that Jesus Christ has commanded us not to tolerate or get along with our enemies, but to actually love them!

Here's the toughest pill to swallow: I'm a red-blooded American military veteran who has spent his entire adult life in the business of protecting other Americans. So naturally when terrorists shoot up a school or threaten our way of life, I get angry. Those who shoot our children and kill our citizens and soldiers aren't human, they're vile scum of the earth. But that's not really true is it? Each human being, no matter how much I demonize them, scripturally is a human being who is one of God's children. And while I like things to be so black and white when deciding what and who is good and evil, it just isn't so. Nothing is black and white. Not only is the human race divided in a thousand different ways, Christianity is divided by its own people because many are unwilling to forgive. Jesus was nailed to the cross when he looked at his executioners and forgave them. There was no doubt that Jesus loved his enemies. Following a mass church shooting in South Carolina, I read first-hand accounts of the surviving members who not only prayed for their murdered church-family, but they prayed for forgiveness and mercy for the shooter. No one questioned that they were following Christ's commandment to us.

Loving your enemy does not mean inviting them over for BBQ and a card game. It doesn't mean we excuse their behavior. But it does mean we forgive them. It means we trust that God will be both just and merciful. Forgiveness begins with prayer. As C.S. Lewis wrote, "Prayer doesn't change God, prayer changes me."

A sk yourself this question: "Why should I go to church?" Each of your individual answers will vary greatly. But there is likely one commonality that we share: the desire to grow in our relationship with God. But all of us, at times, restrain ourselves from receiving God's grace, the very grace that strengthens that relationship. We do this by shamefully clinging to our sin. Sometimes we don't even know we're doing it. Why do we do this? The Old Testament tells us that, in order to be restored to being good people, we must pay a penalty for our sins. When we try to pay that penalty on our own, we become overwhelmed. When we become overwhelmed, our hearts and minds work against us. It's like a credit card bill that we just can't get paid off. This didn't work in Moses' time or any time thereafter. Thus, there is need for a Savior. In his second letter to the early church in Corinth, Paul goes on to explain the error in this Old Testament response to a New Testament matter.

2 Corinthians 3:12-4:2:

3:12 Since, then, we have such a hope, we act with great boldness, 13 not like Moses, who put a veil over his face to keep the people of Israel from gazing at the end of the glory that was being set aside. 14 But their minds were hardened. Indeed, to this very day, when they hear the reading of the old covenant, that same veil is still there, since only in Christ is it set aside. 15 Indeed, to this very day whenever Moses is read, a veil lies over their minds; 16 but when one turns to the Lord, the veil is removed. 17 Now the Lord is the Spirit, and where the Spirit of the Lord is, there is freedom. 18 And all of us, with unveiled faces, seeing the glory of the Lord as though reflected in a mirror, are being transformed into the same image from one degree of glory to another; for this comes from the Lord, the Spirit.

4:1 Therefore, since it is by God's mercy that we are engaged in this ministry, we do not lose heart. 2 We have renounced the shameful things that one hides; we refuse to practice cunning or to falsify God's word; but by the open statement of the truth we commend ourselves to the conscience of everyone in the sight of God.

Paul was always passionate about preaching the cross. He emphasized our daily need for Christ, but also how our individual lives help spread the message of the gospel. In this passage, he makes reference to our Old Testament reading and points out that Moses wore a veil over his face because his own glory was fading after facing God. Moses has just talked one-on-one with God, and has just learned these new commandments. Most, if not all, of these commandments had already been broken by most of the people there at the bottom of Mt. Sinai.

One of the hardest things I had to do in answering my call to ministry was what I refer to today as "removing the veil." When I had finally decided to answer my call to ministry and seek the approval of the Board of Ordained Ministry, I had to submit to a series of interviews that seemed to go on and on. In each of these interviews I had to share many of my most intimate, personal spiritual beliefs and practices. And each time I interviewed they coaxed me into discussing my things of my past. I was fairly ashamed of that part. I wanted them to think I was this great, strong person who avoided sin, so I was less forthcoming about it at first. That was my veil. I had this human natured belief that my greatness was based on my not having sinned, when in all actually, greatness comes from surrender, repentance, and accepting God's grace and forgiveness. Taking off the veil means trusting that Christ has paid that debt of our sins. God gave to us the Holy Trinity of the Father, Son, and Holy Spirit because the Old Testament ways weren't working. And even with the Trinity, even with all the grace that God has given us, even though we might be able to forgive others, we often still don't forgive ourselves. We keep that veil over our face, trying to hide our sins and convince the world that everything is fine.

One great thing about old pastors is that they know a lot of stuff. God has been working through them longer than I've been alive. So when they do stuff, I pay attention. So I'm going to share something that I picked up from a veteran pastor—something that has really helped me.

- Place your hands in a prayer position.
- Close your eyes.
- Try to imagine all the sin and shame and guilt that you have.
- Place it all in your hands.
- Don't let go yet.

Pray this prayer: Gracious and Merciful God, in my hands I have placed all of my sins. Lord, these sins have weighed me down and kept me from fully receiving your grace. I come to you now, seeking your mercy, and trust you to take these sins from me. When I release these sins to you, I will no longer be burdened by them, and I will have lifted my veil for you.

- Now, open your hands and release your sin, shame, and guilt to God. Amen.

"Tempt Me Not"

his past week we started the Lenten season. Christians around the world have faithfully given up something they are fond of until Holy Week and replaced it with devotion to God. This tradition reflects Christ's own fasting in the wilderness for forty days, being tempted by Satan, and not wavering in his tests of faith. So, following Ash Wednesday we create our own "temptation" as a testament to our faith. We do it as a show of solidarity in our trust in God.

It's great to give up sodas or video games or junk food, whatever the case is. It's healthy, and if you're doing it right you're replacing it with a devotion to God...prayer, meditation, scripture reading, something.

Luke 4:1-13:

4:1 Jesus, full of the Holy Spirit, returned from the Jordan and was led by the Spirit in the wilderness, 2 where for forty days he was tempted by the devil. He ate nothing at all during those days, and when they were over, he was famished. 3 The devil said to him, "If you are the Son of God, command this stone to become a loaf of bread." 4 Jesus answered him, "It is written, 'One does not live by bread alone.'"

5 Then the devil led him up and showed him in an instant all the kingdoms of the world. 6 And the devil said to him, "To you I will give their glory and all this authority; for it has been given over to me, and I give it to anyone I please. 7 If you, then, will worship me, it will all be yours." 8 Jesus answered him, "It is written,

'Worship the Lord your God,

and serve only him.'"

9 Then the devil took him to Jerusalem, and placed him on the pinnacle of the temple, saying to him, "If you are the Son of God, throw yourself down from here, 10 for it is written,

'He will command his angels concerning you,

to protect you,'

11 and

'On their hands they will bear you up,

so that you will not dash your foot against a stone.'"

12 Jesus answered him, "It is said, 'Do not put the Lord your God to the test.'" 13 When the devil had finished every test, he departed from him until an opportune time.

In this story Luke describes Jesus being tempted by Satan-first by Satan trying to appear to Jesus' physical needs with a loaf of bread. When that didn't work, Satan tempts Jesus with something spiritual, offering Jesus glory and authority over the whole world, and again Jesus declined.

Physical temptation isn't always easy to overcome, but it's manageable. If we're trying to diet, we refrain from eating certain foods, exercise, and so on. Let me tell you a story about Michael. Michael was morbidly obese, weighing in at 617 pounds. His doctor told him that if he didn't lose weight and start watching his diet and cholesterol, he would be dead in a year or two. Michael's biggest problem was that he would overeat, and it was junk food at that. It was Michael's addiction. He finally made a decision that he was going to fight to live, he was going to resist temptation and defeat the hold that eating had on him. For three years, every time Michael got hungry, he got up, walked three miles to Walmart to buy fresh fruit and vegetables, and walked three miles back home, and incredibly Michael lost a total of 391 pounds. I saw a picture that was taken of this guy at the gym a couple years ago and he's pretty buff now. This is an example of resisting physical temptation.

But what about spiritual temptation? This one's a little harder because sometimes we don't even recognize that it is temptation. I think one of the most dangerous spiritual temptations is to believe the heresy of others. We sometimes find ourselves tempted to believe perversions of scripture and God's intentions because it was told to us in a manner that fits what we want to hear. This is especially dangerous. Another particularly dangerous spiritual booby-trap has to do with money. We're often fooled that more money is a good thing. Here's an eye-opener: I was listening to a speech from a United Methodist Bishop in Africa recently. If you weren't aware, the African continent has had the fasted growing concentration of United Methodist and Catholic churches of anywhere in the world, and building congregations at a rate two and a half times faster than here in America. During this speech, he said that American Christians were too dependent on money to ensure success, pointing out that while we're planning fundraisers and passing around the offering plates, they were volunteering themselves the way the disciples in the early church did to build their ministries. He even stated that it is somewhat insulting to them that we believe we can simply send money to them money and call it a "ministry." Trying to buy our way into the favor of the Lord is called *simony*, a term that refers to Simon Magus in the Book of Acts who was trying to purchase the power of the Holy Spirit. We find ourselves tempted to seek out more money, and when we have more money, we continue to seek out more money. Money sounds good, but it's a dangerous thing. Spiritual temptations.

Some spiritual temptations consume our lives when we find ourselves in a situation that we believe we can't get out of. We become so overwhelmed or afraid that we are tempted to just give up. And I think that's when Satan just has a field day with us, when we feel worthless, sad, and angry. Spiritual temptations.

With all these temptations there is one truth that can shield us, and it's found in the Book of Romans 10:8-13.

10:8 "The word is near you, on your lips and in your heart"

(that is, the word of faith that we proclaim); 9 because if you confess with your lips that Jesus is Lord and believe in your heart that God raised him from the dead, you will be saved. 10 For one believes with the heart and so is justified, and one confesses with the mouth and so is saved. 11 The scripture says, "No one who believes in him will be put to shame." 12 For there is no distinction between Jew and Greek; the same Lord is Lord of all and is generous to all who call on him. 13 For, "Everyone who calls on the name of the Lord shall be saved."

This is the word of God, this is truth. With this truth we can overcome any temptation.

"Shamrock: For St. Patrick's Day"

One of my favorite holidays observed is Saint Patrick's Day. Unfortunately this day has been commercialized and is largely associated with drinking and partying, when this day was originally meant to honor the life and works of Saint Patrick. So just who was Saint Patrick? He is a patron saint of Ireland. Before reaching sainthood, Patrick was a missionary and bishop in the Roman Catholic Church. Most of what we know about him comes from his autobiography titled *"Confessio,"* which as you might have guessed translates to 'confession.' Interestingly enough, Patrick wasn't even Irish. And in the beginning, Patrick didn't even really believe in God. In the 5th century when Patrick was about sixteen years old, he was kidnapped by Irish pirates from his home in what later became Scotland. He was brought to Ireland and forced into slavery, and would spend six years there before escaping from his master and persuading a ship captain to take him along. He eventually made his way back home. After returning home, Patrick became a priest, following in the footsteps of his father and grandfather. He accredits his faith to his captivity, praying to God for freedom, and later had a vision where he was told to expand his ministry to Ireland.

A number of years go by and Patrick's ministry has grown, having been appointed bishop. He is led to return to Ireland to convert the Irish pagans to Christianity. At that time the Celts practiced what's known as *polytheism*, meaning they worshipped multiple gods. Patrick has overwhelming success in converting them. You may have heard stories about Saint Patrick driving out all the snakes in

67

Ireland. What many folks don't realize is that since the last ice age, there have never been any snakes in Ireland. This was actually a reference to his conversion of the druids and his conquest replacing Celtic paganism with Christianity. He has an entourage of disciples who follow him, many of them converts. Monasteries and churches begin to pop up all over Ireland and Patrick begins commissioning new clergy to lead the congregations.

What's especially impressive is his ability to teach the pagans of the concept of the Holy Trinity. Any missionary will tell you that this is one of the most difficult theologies to explain to non-Christians. I mean, I have a hard time getting some church-going folks to understand it. Ephesians 4:4-6 says, *"There is one body and one Spirit, just as you were called to the one hope of your calling, one Lord, one faith, one baptism, one God and Father of all, who is above all and through all and in all."* How can one God be the Father, the Son, and the Holy Spirit all at the same time? Patrick's explanation became Ireland's trademark, one that we still see today.

The shamrock—this three-leafed clover was a teaching tool for Christianity 1,500 years ago. Three leaves: one representing the Father, one representing the Son, and one representing the Holy Spirit-all connected by one central stem, representing God. Three distinctive separate parts, yet all *one* clover.

I've spent some time thinking about what my trademark might be for teaching others about Holy Trinity. I open worship services with a reminder of God's goodness. I note that Scripture readings do, in fact, contain the word of God. These are good, but I haven't quite nailed down my "shamrock." But like Saint Patrick, each of us have a personal calling to serve God.

Philippians 3:17-4:1:

3:17 Join together in following my example, brothers and sisters, and just as you have us as a model, keep your eyes on those who live as we do.18 For, as I have often told you before and now tell you again even with tears, many live as enemies of the cross of Christ. 19 Their destiny is destruction, their god is their stomach, and their glory is in their shame. Their mind is set on earthly things. 20 But our citizenship is in heaven. And we eagerly await a Savior from there, the Lord Jesus Christ, 21 who, by the power that enables him to bring everything under his control, will transform our lowly bodies so that they will be like his glorious body.

4 Therefore, my brothers and sisters, you whom I love and long for, my joy and crown, stand firm in the Lord in this way, dear friends!

Friends, we don't need a shamrock to teach others about Christ. Living as Christians is a teaching tool in itself. Parents, your children are watching you. Children, your friends are watching you. Each one of us is someone's image of the Christian faith. Green beer and rowdy parades are not representative of Saint Patrick's ministry or his miraculous life. Let us honor Saint Patrick as fellow Christians who have been called to serve Christ.

"Justice or Justified"

Based on your own experiences, finish this sentence: "I don't go to church because _____."

There's a lot of possible ways to finish this sentence. We've heard them all. "Churches are full of hypocrites....I've done too many bad things...I don't like to get up early on Sunday." Often times we wonder where these stigmas come from, we wonder why they feel that way.

So let me tell you about Gerald. Gerald was a data analyst for a Fortune 500 company. He was not married and lived alone in a small house. Gerald was addicted to child pornography. Gerald knew what he did was about as wrong and deplorable as anything he could imagine, but he let his addiction consume him nonetheless. One early Saturday morning, police showed up at Gerald's house with a search warrant. They seized Gerald's computers, photo albums, DVD's and video cassettes, and they placed Gerald under arrest. But Gerald had been clever enough to leave very little evidence of his crimes, knowing that he could easily be arrested. He used his knowledge of computers to cover his tracks, and the only crime Gerald was convicted of was a software piracy charge, which bought him eighteen months in a federal prison. Two things happened to Gerald while he was in prison: 1) he decided that he was going to break free of his addiction, and 2) he surrendered his life back to Jesus Christ. Gerald was released from prison and immediately began attending a church from his hometown. Only the pastor and a few members of the congregation would speak to him, and he sat alone in a church pew.

Now, I have to admit that I did not like the idea of a predator like Donald being in a place where my children attended church. What I liked even less was that I had been the investigator on the case in which Donald had been arrested and I knew of crimes that he'd committed that he was never convicted of. At the time, I was unable to accept to Donald as a part of the body of Christ. I was unable to love Donald. Many folks were. It would be years later that I came to understand that the spiritual problem did not lie with Donald, it lied within me. Paul's words in his 2nd letter to the Corinthians reiterates Christ's instructions to his disciples.

2 Corinthians 5:16-21.

5:16 So from now on we regard no one from a worldly point of view. Though we once regarded Christ in this way, we do so no longer.17 Therefore, if anyone is in Christ, the new creation has come: The old has gone, the new is here! 18 All this is from God, who reconciled us to himself through Christ and gave us the ministry of reconciliation: 19 that God was reconciling the world to himself in Christ, not counting people's sins against them. And he has committed to us the message of reconciliation. 20 We are therefore Christ's ambassadors, as though God were making his appeal through us. We implore you on Christ's behalf: Be reconciled to God. 21 God made him who had no sin to be sin for us, so that in him we might become the righteousness of God.

Donald passed away before I would be able to reconcile my feelings towards him. After a while I felt a bit of shame that I was not able to overcome my human feelings for him and love him the way Christ has commanded.

The truth is that we are, quite often, hypocritical in our thinking when it comes to other people's sins. Yes, there's some truth in the stigma. We pray for others. In fact, every week the congregation prays the Lord's Prayer, and we recite the words "Forgive us our trespasses, as we forgive those who trespass against us." Yet, there are many who we fail to forgive. We're often okay with forgiving some sins: taking the Lord's name in vain, doubt, getting drunk. We're even okay with forgiving some of the more serious stuff like, infidelity and drug addiction. But are we really forgiving all that we are commanded? What about organized crime...what about murder? Would you sit in a church pew with a former member of al-Qaeda who killed Christians because of their beliefs, but had since become Christian himself? Could you love that person? Would you invite that person into your home? If the answer is no, then we know what we need to work on.

If we are to believe that Christ died for the sin of humanity, and that we have been forgiven, then we have to understand that Christ died for all sin, and that those who seek forgiveness are truly forgiven. We have to understand that God's justifying grace is sufficient for Him to forgive us, and what is sufficient for God is certainly sufficient for us. We understand that humanity was created in God's image, and that image becomes distorted by sin, but God's justifying grace restores us to that image through Christ's death on the cross.

Part of chaplaincy involves going into the mission and assessing what's called 'pastoral triage,' which is method of categorizing 'who needs God the most' and in which manner. For example, if I respond to a call to visit a person in the hospital who is dying and the family is distraught, that's obviously going to be a priority over getting a phone call that someone's boyfriend cheated on them. Both are important, but one requires priority over the other. All Christians are tasked with being able to assess pastoral triage. Those who need God's love the most urgently are seldom those who have good reputations, or have made good decisions, or have a broad knowledge of Scripture. As disciples we have a mission to extend the church to them, to welcome them, to love them as we are commanded. Paul, who wrote the letters known to us as 'the epistles' was once like the former al-Qaeda member I mentioned. Before his conversion to Christianity, Paul was a notorious persecutor of Christians, then known as Saul, hunting them down and subjecting them to torture and even murder. These kinds of sinners are exactly the kind of people who Jesus kept company with-killers, prostitutes, thieves...as well as the poor and wealthy alike. Luke 15:1-3 says, "15 Now all the dishonest tax collectors and sinners were coming near to listen to him. 2 And the Pharisees and the scribes were grumbling and saying, "This fellow welcomes sinners and eats with them."

In our dealings with other people, we need to constantly pose to ourselves this question, "Am I acting as Christ would have acted, with love and compassion for my neighbor, or am I the judgmental Pharisee, grumbling about other sinners?"

When we think of Jesus we often imagine a peaceful, quiet Jesus. We see images of Jesus doing peaceful things in artwork. Jesus preaches about peaceful things in Scripture. But the truth is that Jesus was quite bold, oftentimes even defiant. Today we celebrate Palm Sunday, and examine one of Jesus' boldest moves in the Gospel. Jesus is on his way to Jerusalem and stops at Mount Olivet. He tells two of his disciples to go to a nearby village and retrieve an unbroken colt. He tells them that if anyone asks, tell them, "It's for the Lord." So these two disciples go and retrieve this unbroken colt for Jesus. Now this thing has never been ridden, it's young and inexperienced, possibly even a bit wild. This colt is not fully grown, certainly not the type of steed you'd ride into battle. So what happens next?

Luke 19:35-40:

19:35 Then they brought him to Jesus. And they threw their own clothes on the colt, and they set Jesus on him. 36 And as He went, many spread their clothes on the road.

37 Then, as He was now drawing near the descent of the Mount of Olives, the whole multitude of the disciples began to rejoice and praise God with a loud voice for all the mighty works they had seen, 38 saying:

" 'Blessed is the King who comes in the name of the Lord!'

Peace in heaven and glory in the highest!"

39 And some of the Pharisees called to Him from the crowd, "Teacher, rebuke Your disciples."

74

40 But He answered and said to them, "I tell you that if these should keep silent, the stones would immediately cry out."

So Jesus rides this ridiculous little colt through the west gates of Jerusalem. He has a parade of disciples in front of him, waving palm leaves, which was a Jewish celebratory tradition originating in the Old Testament. There are crowds of disciples gathering, cheering for Jesus. Now, this sight surely has to be pretty remarkable considering the Messiah is riding into town on some wimpy livestock. So why is this bold? Because Jesus is drawing a line in the sand. But we have to know the backstory to fully understand.

So, the same time each year during the Passover, Herod Antipas, would ride into Jerusalem through the east gates with his military forces. Herod Antipas was the ruler of Galilee and Perea, his authority was confirmed by the Roman Empire, he was educated in Rome, and was not a particularly nice person. This is the same Herod who had executed Jesus' cousin, John the Baptist. Herod would ride into Jerusalem this time each year, on a mighty warhorse, in a show of Roman military force to suppress any potential challenges to Roman domination in the city. And on this same day Jesus rides into town from the opposite direction, riding a borrowed, wimpy donkey-colt, while being escorted by a bunch of disciples armed with palm branches. Make no mistake, Jesus' mission is demonstrate the mighty kingship of God and to offer peace. Now this act seems much bolder. His disciples recognize what's going on, they cheer him. The Pharisees warn Jesus to tell them to shut up, and Jesus says, "I tell you that if these should keep silent, the stones would immediately cry out!" Again Jesus has made a bold move with that statement. You see, the meaning behind the 'stones crying out' refers to a revolt.

Jesus doesn't have to walk around with his chest puffed out to be bold. But it's us, the human race, who recognizes and responds to such behavior. There are three types of Christian disciples: you have people who claim to be Christian but do nothing beyond making the claim; you have luke-warm Christians who claim the title, go to church, tithe, and try to get by in life with as little difficulty as possible; and then you have the bold Christians. This is what we should strive to be: bold in our faith, bold in our service to God, bold in our witness and prayer life. I'm not afraid to say, "Yeah, I'm a depraved sinner, I've carried this burden or that burden, but that's alright now because Jesus Christ has become Lord and Savior of my life!" I shout it to the world!

But simply shouting about our faith isn't bold enough. The Hebrew meaning of wisdom means both divine knowledge and divine action. We need to be bold in our Christian actions. Jesus was bold. Jesus stood up to a tyrannical government to teach them godly ways. Would you stand up against a government that did not practice Christian values? Jesus made friends with people who were poor, who were outcasts, who were sinners. He showed them love and mercy. Would you befriend someone like that? Jesus forgave the people who tortured and condemned him. Could you forgive someone who planned to kill you? In fact, Jesus was so bold that he died on the cross in front of scores of witnesses, and was subsequently resurrected from the dead to show people that God can defeat sin and death? Have you become dead to sin and risen again in the light of Christ Jesus? Friends, being bold in our faith means taking bold action. Baptism is a bold action for Christ. Mission is a bold action for Christ. Standing up against that which Christ condemned, even if it means being ridiculed by others, is a bold action for Christ. Live bold for a bold Savior friends.

What a glorious time to be alive! We live in a nation of freedoms. Medical science has developed cures and vaccinations to end horrible diseases. Our economy in the United States is the largest and strongest in the world. And forget the United States, let's talk about Texas! I bet there's a few of us here that can you what a blessing it is to be a Texan. I was doing my taxes a few weeks ago and I remember thinking to myself, "Man, am I sure glad we don't have to pay state income tax here." We've got Bluebonnets, and awesome lakes and beaches, and the Alamo, and some of the best universities in the world. But even beyond Texas and America, end even the Earth for that matter, we've entered this period of advanced space exploration. Humans put a spacecraft on Mars. I don't know about you, but that is amazing to me. Just a couple of weeks ago we got our very first picture of a black hole. Honestly, up until that time I didn't know we hadn't already taken any pictures of black holes, but nonetheless I was glad to have lived during the time where that first photo was revealed. The study into this black hole, now with photographic evidence that it exists, has also scientifically proven a number of theoretics about space-time, such as Einstein's 'Theory of Relativity' and the First Law of Thermodynamics (being that energy can neither be created nor destroyed).

What a blessing to have lived to see such times! And to have known such great people! Did you ever think about that: That if you'd been born in any other period of time, you wouldn't know the people that you know. We like to think.

We like explanations and scientific breakdowns. For some reason humanity needs that assurance, not only to know that something exists, but an explanation of how it exists. While ideology works well for people like scientists, and investigators, and doctors, it creates a significant hurdle for members of the clergy. Especially on this day. How in God's Kingdom are we supposed to understand how Jesus was resurrected?

And if we can't explain it, what does that mean about the rest of our faith? Logic and reason are often the enemies of creativity and imagination. For example, if I tell a child that Jesus brought back a man from the dead, that child will likely believe it to be so. If I tell the same bible story to an adult, logic and reason kick in: "dead things stay, right?" Our experiences and knowledge in these adult brains of ours tell us that unnatural acts are against logic and reason.

We've heard the Easter story. Jesus was tortured, crucified, and dead, and three days later Mary Magdalene, Mary the mother of James, and Salome go to His tomb and find it empty. Priests, pastors, and evangelists around the world would preach that this is the moment that history rejoices. "Hallelujah! Hallelujah! He has risen! Hallelujah!" But that's not the case. It's not even the case in Scripture. You everyone's logic kicks in. The women who first enter the tomb, the disciples, the Romans...everyone knows that a dead body cannot come back to life. And so, even in Scripture, people ask the question, "How would that be possible?"

Since that time, we have yet to have a defined explanation of how Jesus Christ was resurrected from death. And while you might be sitting here expecting me to give a preacher's rendition of a scripted answer that was taught in

79

some theology class, you would be mistaken.   You see friends, we cannot explain God. We cannot explain how God works. I can't tell you why God didn't intervene and stop Eve from picking that apple. I can't explain how God created the Heavens and the Earth. And I can't explain how Jesus was resurrected from the dead. If it could be explained, it couldn't be called faith anymore, it would be called science.

I've been asked many times by many people, "Do you really believe the stuff in the bible?" I tell them, "Yes, I do." And usually they'll follow up by asking, "How can you believe that?" Friends, the short answer is that years ago I chose to believe in the authority of the Scriptures. That was a decision I made of my own free will and accord. Faith doesn't come naturally, we have to make that decision for ourselves.

A scary trend began several decades ago, primarily in Western Europe and the United States. Christians have started to reject key elements of Christianity and have begun to adopt more Unitarian beliefs. In fact, in a survey that was conducted in the United Kingdom earlier this year, several thousand church-going Christians were polled about their beliefs. Get this: over 40% stated that they did believe Jesus was literally resurrected from the dead. And of that 40%, 18% said they did not believe that Jesus Christ had any divine powers at all. Can that 18% even call themselves Christians at that point?

To those 40%, and whoever else might fit in that category: ask me how I know the resurrection happened.

I know because Jesus was crucified somewhere around the year of 33 A.D. and it's now 2019 and I see the work of Jesus Christ each and every day. I just saw the Notre Dame Cathedral enveloped in flames, and when the fire was out the cross on the altar remained unharmed. I see people sharing God's love with other people. I see the mission that Jesus Christ set forth for us being undertaken by people of all walks of life. I see people draw hope from Christ. I see the words of Jesus give peace to people at the end of their lives. I know what Jesus has done for me, and that He lives within my heart. That, friends, is all the science and explanation I need. The rest of it is what we call, "faith."

Einstein didn't live long enough to see the picture of the black hole that proved his 'Theory of Relativity'. I will likely not live long enough to see any definitive explanation of the resurrection beyond the Scriptures. Einstein did not see his work as useless. And I have never felt like any part of my ministry was a waste of time, nor do I believe that about the past 2000 years of Christianity. Faith is a choice, make it. Hallelujah! He is risen!

In Revelation 5:11-14, John writes,

5:11 Then I looked, and I heard the voice of many angels around the throne, the living creatures, and the elders; and the number of them was ten thousand times ten thousand, and thousands of thousands, 12 saying with a loud voice:

"Worthy is the Lamb who was slain

To receive power and riches and wisdom,

And strength and honor and glory and blessing!"

13 And every creature which is in heaven and on the earth and under the earth and such as are in the sea, and all that are in them, I heard saying:

"Blessing and honor and glory and power

Be to Him who sits on the throne,

And to the Lamb, forever and ever!"

14 Then the four living creatures said, "Amen!" And the twenty-four elders fell down and worshiped Him who lives forever and ever.

Sometimes people are surprised that after being a cop for so many I went into ministry. I tell them that's it's really not all that different. In fact, that's one thing I love about working in the criminal justice system is how similar to religion it is. I mean think about it: there's good, there's evil, there's judgement, all that stuff that's talked about in the Bible I get to see in action all the time. So quite often I get asked what it is that I do as deputy constable. Like other law enforcement agencies, we go on 911 calls and write tickets and all that stuff. But those aren't our primary duties. Primarily the Constable's Office is the enforcement branch of the court system. When a judge issues a court order, and that order's not followed, we enforce the order. We serve court documents to people and businesses. We find people who don't want to be found. One additional duty that is assigned to me at my department is serving arrest warrants. This is the thing that most folks find interesting. In the scope of what I do, it requires the least amount technical training, it's all about finding a person and bringing them to jail.

So what happens when a judge issues a warrant and it comes across my desk? I start by doing a little research on the person I'm going to arrest, seeing if they've been in our jail before or if they have any other warrants. I'll check out their Facebook page, find out who their family members are. You'd be surprised how much I can find out about you in about five minutes of sitting at my desk. Once I've got an idea of where I'm going to look for this person, start knocking on doors. Sometimes the people are there, sometimes I talk to their family, sometimes I just have to leave a card on the door. But rest assured that when I find them, they have to go to jail. It is non-negotiable. People will try to get me to come back at a more convenient time, or say they'll turn themselves in tomorrow if I'll just let them go today. It doesn't work that way. When I find them, they go to jail. Such is the law. Those who flee or attempt to elude me are classified as fugitives. They will be caught at some point.

Friends, Death has a warrant for our arrest...every one of us. And Death will catch us. And when Death catches us it doesn't matter if we are ready to go, if we're happy, if we're expecting it, if we're sitting in the bleachers watching our kids or grandkids playing a little league game...we have to go when Death catches us. Each one of us will experience this differently. For some this will be peaceful and swift. For others it may be an unpleasant, even painful experience. The chances are that we're not trying to think about this. We eat healthy, we stay in shape, we go to the doctor, we don't act recklessly. It's safe to say that we avoid death. We are fugitives from death. So when death catches us and we die, what will happen? What questions will we ask as we grab at our chest and take our last breath? Have I done enough? Did I live a good life? Did I love people? Did they love me? Will I be forgiven?

Well, just like other fugitives, after we're caught there will be a judgement. Scripture tells us that we'll be judged on many merits throughout the course of our mortal lives, but none so more than that of faith and good works. And if you're wondering if you've been good enough to get a reduced sentence, let me make it clear to you. You haven't. None of us have. Therefore we must enlist the help of the only defense attorney that can save us, Jesus the Christ. And he specializes in grace.

The Easter story and the months following were not about celebrating a Risen Savior. The Bible doesn't tell us of the disciples hiding Easter eggs while their children pig out on chocolate bunnies. No, this was a period of disbelief, when Christ had trouble even getting the disciples to recognize Him. Jesus kept appearing to them, having conversations with them, but in a number of instances they either didn't recognize Him or they believed it to be some kind of parlor trick. Jesus had to let them feel Him, He had to make a number of appearances, He had to perform these great miracles...ultimately, it took repetition. There it is, the word of the day: repetition. Why do need to put Jesus into our lives, into daily routines every single day? Why do we come to church services? Why do we read the same Bible over and over? Repetition.

It's okay to have questions. It's okay to not understand everything about God, and Jesus, and the afterlife. But we should recognize Christ in our lives, and being repetitive in our faith helps us do that. When we have Christ as our Savior, we will find our pardon from sin and death.

"Are You Listening To Me: A Mother's Day Message"

Today is a special day: it's the day we honor our mothers. And why not? I mean, our mothers have done so many great things for us. Mom nurtures us, mom protects us, mom teaches us. Where would we be without mom? And for some of us, mom was a role filled by someone other than our biological mother. What a great gift that is! Speaking of gifts...did we give our mothers a gift today? Well guess what...today we're going to undertake a short but important mission. We're going to give our mothers a special gift. Yep, even those of you whose mothers have passed on to be with the Lord. We'll come back to that.

I can remember so many times I just didn't listen to my mom. Now that I'm older I really wish I had. I wish I had done my best in school. I wish I'd taken all those naps she told me to take when I was little, I'd love the chance to get all those opportunities back! I wish I'd stayed away from junk food...dieting is tough. One thing that my mother told me was something probably all of you heard before: "Whatever you do in life, be happy." Now that seems like a pretty simple concept, right? So why is it that this seems to be such a challenge for some folks?

Jesus had trouble getting people to listen to Him sometimes, too. In fact, Jesus told the world all kinds of things that some people still don't hear.

John 10:22-30.

10:22 Now it was the Feast of Dedication in Jerusalem, and it was winter. 23 And Jesus walked in the temple, in

Solomon's porch. 24 Then the Jews surrounded Him and said to Him, "How long do You keep us in doubt? If You are the Christ, tell us plainly."

25 Jesus answered them, "I told you, and you do not believe. The works that I do in My Father's name, they bear witness of Me. 26 But you do not believe, because you are not of My sheep, as I said to you. 27 My sheep hear My voice, and I know them, and they follow Me. 28 And I give them eternal life, and they shall never perish; neither shall anyone snatch them out of My hand. 29 My Father, who has given them to Me, is greater than all; and no one is able to snatch them out of My Father's hand. 30 I and My Father are one."

In this piece of Scripture you have a number of Jews who have approached Jesus during a public festival at Hanukah as they're rededicating the Jewish temple. And they're asking Him, "Hey, are you the Messiah?" Jesus says, "I told you, and you do not believe." He even makes reference to Himself as the shepherd that's prophesied in Ezekiel 34:23, "I will set up over them one shepherd..." And these people continue not to believe Him. In fact, they pick up stones to stone Jesus with.

Now at times I was a stubborn kid, but I never thought about stoning my mother. But there were things that mom told me that I refused to listen to. And for the most part, my stubbornness would come back to bite me. Just think about how much better the world would be if we'd...just...listen....to Christ. Jesus knows best, friends. Think about how much love there'd be in the world if we were all sheep in the Shepherd's flock.

Moms are sort of like Jesus, or Jesus is sort of like moms, I don't know which. But what I do know is that mom and Jesus both love us, protect us, guide us, nurture us, and give us life. So what are some things we can give back to both mom and Jesus?

Let's start with affection. We need to show them some love. It's a little tough for some of us, I'm not a particularly affectionate person. But showing mom love can come in many forms. Find something she'll like. Showing Jesus affection is probably easier, you're doing it right now. Pray in His name, love Him and share that love with others. That's a few good ways to show affection to Jesus.

Next you can give them affirmation. Show your mom that you've learned from her, that all the time and love she's invested in you has been worth-while. The chances are that you turned out differently than your mom had imagined at some point. So let her know that there's a part of her that you still carry. Affirm to Jesus that you have put your faith into Him and will be His disciple. Many people know the Apostle's Creed by heart, but what would your creed say if you wrote out your own Affirmation of Faith? Try it!

Your next gift is appreciation. When's the last time you thanked your mom? Hopefully it wasn't last Mother's Day. Friends, mom gave you life! Thank her for it! Thank her for everything she did for you! Then thank Jesus! Thank them, you'll never know how much grace they both gave to you throughout your life!

Finally, give them the gift of happiness. Not theirs. Yours. A long time ago I realized that success had nothing to do with college degrees or money in my bank account. It had to do with happiness. For a moment, each day, reflect on the things in your life that bring you happiness. We can't be happy all the time, but we can dedicate a moment of our lives to happiness. Try to make this a habit. As a parent, we worry about our children, we know all the struggles and dangers that they will face, and all we want in the end is for them to be happy. And Jesus wants that for us too. Commit a moment of your day to being happy. These are simple gifts that mean more than gold and jewels. They are timeless gifts for the living and for the Saints. May God bless all the mothers this day!

E ach year on Memorial Day we recognize and celebrate the brave men and women of the armed forces who sacrificed their lives for us. Many people will get together with family and friends for food and good times. As someone who has served, and continues to serve, I tell you that I'm perfectly okay with Americans celebrating the holiday this way. Our way of life, these liberties we enjoy, they don't come free. It's important to remember that there are a number of families who spend Memorial Day at the graveside of a loved one who made the ultimate sacrifice.

During the American Civil War, the Confederate Army commandeered the Washington Race Track in Charleston, North Carolina and repurposed it as a makeshift prison for captured Union soldiers. More than 260 of these Union prisoners died of disease and exposure and were buried in a shallow mass grave in the infield of the track. Later when the Confederacy retreated after the fall of Charleston, many of the newly freed slaves remained in the city. One of their first undertakings was to give proper burials to the dead soldiers. They exhumed the bodies and reinterred them in a proper cemetery. Then, on May 1, 1865 the New York Tribune and the Charleston Courier both reported that a crowd of 10,000 people, comprised mostly of freed slaves and Christian missionaries, staged a parade around the race track, singing songs, preaching, and honoring the soldiers who gave their lives. This was the earliest documented celebration of Memorial Day, and the first national recognition of the holiday was celebrated at

Arlington National Cemetery on May 30, 1868, where both Union and Confederate troops are buried.

On June 6, 1944 nearly 160,000 Allied troops crossed the English Channel to liberate France from Nazi occupation, held by 51,000 German soldiers. By the end of WWII, over 16 million Allied soldiers had died in combat. These men and women had been sent into battle for a noble cause.

On March 8, 1965 3,500 US Marines came ashore in Da Nang, becoming the first wave over of US combat troops in South Vietnam following many years of political tension. Before the end of the war, the American government would send over 2.7 million to the jungles of Vietnam. 58,318 died, and over 300,000 were wounded in combat. These men and women had been sent into battle for a noble cause.

We fast-forward a few decades to March 20, 2003 when President George W. Bush declared war on international terrorism and the governments that harbored them. This led to a major US invasion of Iraq with an initial coalition force of 309,000. This effort led to the overthrow of Saddam Hussein and his regime, and liberate the Iraqi people from years of tyranny. The war lasted more than eight years, and by the end, 117,961 coalition troops and law enforcement personnel had lost their lives. These men and women had been sent into battle for a noble cause.

Each one of these souls had a sense of duty. They didn't run away. They weren't making millions of dollars doing it. They knew that there was no guarantee of their safe return home. They were sent to far-off places, and they did as they were ordered. Imagine if they had not been sent, and they had not done their duty. I'm fairly convinced that none of the other more recent conflicts would have mattered. If we'd lost WWII, Korea, Vietnam, Iraq, Afghanistan, wouldn't have happened because all of us would be speaking German. Or dead.

As disciples we, too, have marching orders. In fact, we are sent into a spiritual battlefield each and every day. Sometimes our mission is to simply serve our church, sometimes it's to save someone's life, sometimes it's to just live as a disciple in Christ, or perhaps it's the sharing of a special gift. Whatever it is, when God gives us orders, we deploy. Paul describes just such an occasion in Acts 16:9-15.

16:9 ...a vision appeared to Paul in the night. A man of Macedonia stood and pleaded with him, saying, "Come over to Macedonia and help us." 10 Now after he had seen the vision, immediately we sought to go to Macedonia, concluding that the Lord had called us to preach the gospel to them.

11 Therefore, sailing from Tro-as, we ran a straight course to Samothrace, and the next day came to Neapolis, 12 and from there to Philippi, which is the foremost city of that part of Macedonia, a colony. And we were staying in that city for some days. 13 And on the Sabbath day we went out of the city to the riverside, where prayer was customarily made; and we sat down and spoke to the women who met there. 14 Now a certain woman named Lydia heard us. She was a seller of purple from the city of Thy-a-tira, who worshiped God. The Lord opened her heart to heed the things spoken by Paul. 15 And when she and her household were baptized, she begged us, saying, "If you have judged me to be faithful to the Lord, come to my house and stay." So she persuaded us.

Paul recognized that he was being directed by the Spirit to take his ministry to Macedonia. All in all, what happens there doesn't seem too extreme. But let's take a closer look at our text. So Paul is led to Macedonia. There he meets this woman named Lydia. We're told that she's a seller of purple, more specifically meaning she dealt in selling purple clothing dye. And we're told she was a very well-to-do purple dye agent. She was baptized by Paul and converted to Christianity. Now, that happens a lot in Scripture. But in this text, we're actually witnessing the very first conversion of a European. She has become known as Saint Lydia of Thy-a-tira. Because Paul followed his orders. Friends, where is God ordering you to be today? Where is God sending you? Are you listening to the Holy Spirit, and if so, are fulfilling your duty? As we honor our military heroes this Memorial Day, let us honor God every day. Let us courageously stand up for God's noble causes. Because, friends, valor is not only found in far-off battlefields. It's found in the hearts of disciples.

"The Big Tree"

Acts 2:1-21

2:1 When the day of Pentecost had come, they were all together in one place. 2 And suddenly from heaven there came a sound like the rush of a violent wind, and it filled the entire house where they were sitting. 3 Divided tongues, as of fire, appeared among them, and a tongue rested on each of them. 4 All of them were filled with the Holy Spirit and began to speak in other languages, as the Spirit gave them ability.

5 Now there were devout Jews from every nation under heaven living in Jerusalem. 6 And at this sound the crowd gathered and was bewildered, because each one heard them speaking in the native language of each. 7 Amazed and astonished, they asked, "Are not all these who are speaking Galileans? 8 And how is it that we hear, each of us, in our own native language? 9 Parthians, Medes, Elamites, and residents of Mesopotamia, Judea and Cappadocia, Pontus and Asia, 10 Phrygia and Pamphylia, Egypt and the parts of Libya belonging to Cyrene, and visitors from Rome, both Jews and proselytes, 11 Cretans and Arabs—in our own languages we hear them speaking about God's deeds of power." 12 All were amazed and perplexed, saying to one another, "What does this mean?" 13 But others sneered and said, "They are filled with new wine."

14 But Peter, standing with the eleven, raised his voice and addressed them, "Men of Judea and all who live in Jerusalem, let this be known to you, and listen to what I say. 15 Indeed, these are not drunk, as you suppose, for it is only nine o'clock in the morning. 16 No, this is what was spoken through the prophet Joel:

17

'In the last days it will be, God declares,

that I will pour out my Spirit upon all flesh,

> *and your sons and your daughters shall prophesy,*

and your young men shall see visions,

> *and your old men shall dream dreams.*

18 Even upon my slaves, both men and women,

> *in those days I will pour out my Spirit; and they shall prophesy.*

19 And I will show portents in the heaven above

> *and signs on the earth below, blood, and fire, and smoky mist.*

20 The sun shall be turned to darkness

> *and the moon to blood, before the coming of the Lord's great and glorious day.*

21 Then everyone who calls on the name of the Lord shall be saved.'

Oh come upon us, Holy Spirit! We celebrate the Pentecost, the arrival of the Holy Spirit following Christ's Ascension into Heaven. While most Christians have at least a basic understanding of the Holy Spirit, there are those out there who don't understand it. How would you describe the Holy Spirit to someone who was new to the faith, or had never heard the Word before? A safe definition of the Holy Spirit is 'the present activity of God in our midst.' When we feel led by God to do something, to take on a new challenge, or we feel comfort by God, we often refer to this as being 'led by the Spirit.'

Scripture tells us that Christ ascended into Heaven to prepare a place for each of us. But rather than a time of sorrow regarding Christ's departure, this is a time of great joy among believers. And Jesus doesn't just leave us alone, on our own, to fend for ourselves. In His place is this living "representation" that moves us, guides us, helps us be in service to God.

So…the Holy Trinity: three equal forms of God. God the Father. God the Son. God the Holy Spirit. While all three of these are forms of God, we perceive them in three distinctly separate ways. First we have God the Father, the supernatural form of God which we are unable to see, or touch, and so on. This is the Creator. Then we have God the Son, the form of God which was sent to us so that we might better relate, understand, and believe. This is Christ. Last, we have the God the Holy Spirit. But the Holy Spirit is more than simply a "Spirit." This is the natural form of God, meaning that this form of God we can feel, see, sense, and so forth. The Holy Spirit has been described as forces found in nature throughout the New Testament. Matthew, for example, describes a baptism where the Holy Spirit descends as a dove. In our text today the Holy Spirit is described as wind and fire. Elsewhere it's referred to as the 'breath of God.' In fact, the Hebrew word for Spirit is "*ruah*" which literally translates to wind or breath.

These symbols of the Holy Spirit reflect both things that are found in our natural world, and a close relationship with God. Doves, wind, and fire are found in a nature. Breathing is also a very natural act. But think about feeling

96

someone's breath. You typically have to be pretty close to them. Think about leaning in to hear the whisper of someone who trusts you. Imagine the moment immediately following a kiss between lovers. Picture a mother cradling her newborn child. These are times when we would likely feel someone's breath-when we're close and attentive to them.

When the Holy Spirit fills us, moves us, works through us...we are both close to God and in a natural state. And isn't it great when the Holy Spirit moves through us? Think of all the amazing things that we've achieved, all the great ministries, all the love and peace we've felt.

Years ago I was on a Boy Scout hiking trip with Mason. We'd marched for several miles through public US Army Corps of Engineer lands south of Lake Lavon. Along that walking trail lives one of the largest oak trees in Texas. The base of this tree's trunk is roughly ten feet in diameter. The other trees around it looked tiny in comparison. This mighty old oak tree had grown and thrived there for years along the bank of Wilson Creek. It has sufficient water supply, adequate nutrition in the soil, plenty of sunlight, it's shielded from damaging storms by the surrounding trees. The tree is estimated to be between 300-500 years old. This tree clearly stands out from all the others.

It was later while I was walking on a sidewalk in the city I noticed a much smaller oak tree. With concrete streets and sidewalks and buildings surrounding it, this little tree had about a two foot by two foot opening in the concrete where it had been planted. That tree wanted to grow, and it had grown as much as it could until it filled the opening and had cracked and buckled the edges of the concrete around it. It stopped growing. It had been restricted from reaching its potential.

The difference in these two trees is that the big tree is seemingly limitless in its natural, God-given state, while the other one had been restricted by our own devices. Concrete, artificial soil, limited water, buildings blocking out the sunlight. Friends, don't let restrict the Holy Spirit within you. Our missions as disciples can't have concrete slabs, we can't let our light be blocked out by things in which God did not intend. When we see a need, a mission placed before us, we need to set down our roots deep into the ground and be nourished by the Spirit, and watch that mission grow, and grow, and grow. If we spend more time thinking of reasons why we can't do what the Holy Spirit has led us to do, then we're pouring concrete slabs and choking out our spiritual selves. God wants us to send our roots deep, to thrive off of Him, to be strong and secure in His grace. Oh come upon us, Holy Spirit!

W e've all heard the term *"God's law."* Quite often we equate this to the same context as our law, written by our elected officials to govern the land. While this is, in essence, correct, it's so only in part. Like much of the Christian faith, there's always more to it than we might realize. So here's the question we'll set out to answer today: If Jesus Christ was sent to us to create a new covenant and abolish the law, do God's commandments in the Old Testament still apply?

Paul talks about this in his letter to the Galatians in chapter 3:19-29.

3:19 Why then the law? It was added because of transgressions, until the offspring would come to whom the promise had been made; and it was ordained through angels by a mediator. 20 Now a mediator involves more than one party; but God is one.

21 Is the law then opposed to the promises of God? Certainly not! For if a law had been given that could make alive, then righteousness would indeed come through the law. 22 But the scripture has imprisoned all things under the power of sin, so that what was promised through faith in Jesus Christ might be given to those who believe.

23 Now before faith came, we were imprisoned and guarded under the law until faith would be revealed. 24 Therefore the law was our disciplinarian until Christ came, so that we might be justified by faith. 25 But now that faith has come, we are no longer subject to a disciplinarian, 26 for in Christ Jesus you are all children of God through faith. 27 As many of you as were baptized into Christ have clothed yourselves with Christ. 28 There is no longer Jew or Greek, there is no longer slave or free, there is no longer male and female; for all of you are one in Christ Jesus. 29 And if you belong to Christ, then you are Abraham's offspring, heirs according to the promise.

So, in a nutshell, what Paul explains here is that God's original system of government for His children was, in a sense, modified or adapted. So why did God change? He didn't, we did. It makes sense when we compare it to our own system of laws and government.

So think about it: just about every law and rule we have has its roots in the commandments found in the Old Testament. Those same laws have been rewritten and modified thousands of times throughout history, not as a result of a changing God, but as a result of a changing society. Let's take theft for example. Of the well-known Ten Commandments, number eight says, "Thou shalt not steal." This law has been adopted by nearly every government in the world through the course of history. When Texas became a nation, and later a state, its government adopted laws against theft, defining what 'theft' is and providing an appropriate punishment for those found guilty of it. Every couple of years, the laws are reviewed by the state legislature to ensure they are still effective. Several years ago if someone stole something worth $20, they could be issued a ticket rather than be arrested. However if they stole something worth $75, the punishment was classified as more severe and they had to be taken to jail. The legislature reviewed this and increased the ticketable amount of theft to $100. Why? Changes in society, specifically inflation. That same stolen item that was worth $20 ten years ago now costs

$75. To maintain a fair and effective justice system, we decided we didn't want to incarcerate people simply because we had changed the value of something. Now, convey that same principal to all the six-hundred-some-odd commandments of God. As Paul explained, the law is a faith-based system.

A misbelief that many people have is that Christ abolished the Old Testament laws. That is not the case. In Matthew 5:17 Jesus says, "Do not misunderstand why I have come. I did not come to abolish the law of Moses or the writings of the prophets." Instead, as we read earlier in our scripture, Jesus came as a mediator. What does a mediator do? He helps us resolve our issues in a peaceful manner. The problem with the laws of the Old Testament is that we often don't correctly understand them. There's three types of laws that we have we have to recognize.

The first is ceremonial law. A lot of the Old Testament commandments have to do solely with the ritualistic worship practices of Israel that were designed to point them towards the coming Messiah. These laws exist now mostly as a historical factor and bear little relevance to Christians today.

The second is civil law. These are the commandments that were put in place to govern our daily conduct. Since modern society is so different from ancient Israel, these laws cannot be specifically followed. But the principles behind the reasoning remain evident and timeless.

The third law is moral law. These are the commandments that are directly from God and require strict obedience. An example of these are the Ten

Commandments. These are particularly important because they reflect the very nature of God.

Of these three types of Old Testament laws, only a small fraction of them actually apply to modern Christians in relation to our practices since many of them were established for Israelite society before Christ. Since Christ's arrival, we have been emancipated from the strict penalties and practices of the Old Testament laws as evidenced in verse 25. Yes, the laws still matter. If they didn't there would be no need for a Savior.

E very human being who has ever lived has, at some point, found themselves feeling lost, alone, afraid, in some state of despair. Several years ago I got a phone call from an old friend from school, she was completely hysterical to the degree that I could barely understand what she was telling me. It turned out that her husband, whom she had been having marital problems with, had taken his own life. Years of alcohol abuse and untreated depression had led this man to do the unthinkable, leaving behind his estranged wife and children.

Her last words to me over the phone before she hung up were, "Why would God let this happen?"

On December 26, 2015, a freak tornado outbreak swept through north Texas, killing nearly a dozen people, destroying nearly two-hundred homes and businesses, and causing hundreds of millions of dollars in damage. One of the neighborhoods hit hardest was one where another of my friends lived. I sent him a text message to make sure he was ok. He responded telling me that he and his family had taken shelter in the bathroom when the roof was ripped off the house and the second story floor had collapsed on top of them. They had minor injuries, but survived. They lost all of their possessions, including their vehicles.

He texted me, "We lost everything, but God saved us."

Both of these events were very traumatic. Both of these people's faith were tested. The woman in the first story struggled with the idea of religion for a long time after her husband's suicide. The man in the second story struggled with just about every else except his faith as his family put their lives back together. But here's the amazing part: the end result was the same for both of them. God had restored them to a state of wellbeing. Now, you might be thinking, "that's not fair." A person who waivers in their faith in God gets the same benefit as the one who didn't. But what we understand to be fair doesn't necessarily reflect the amazing power of grace.

Revelation 21:1-6:

21:1 Now I saw a new heaven and a new earth, for the first heaven and the first earth had passed away. Also there was no more sea. 2 Then I, John, saw the holy city, New Jerusalem, coming down out of heaven from God, prepared as a bride adorned for her husband. 3 And I heard a loud voice from heaven saying, "Behold, the tabernacle of God is with men, and He will dwell with them, and they shall be His people. God Himself will be with them and be their God. 4 And God will wipe away every tear from their eyes; there shall be no more death, nor sorrow, nor crying. There shall be no more pain, for the former things have passed away."

5 Then He who sat on the throne said, "Behold, I make all things new." And He said to me, "Write, for these words are true and faithful."

6 And He said to me, "It is done! I am the Alpha and the Omega, the Beginning and the End. I will give of the fountain of the water of life freely to him who thirsts.

The final passage in this third major section of Revelation recounts the new creation, a new heaven, and a new earth. The New Jerusalem appears to always be coming down from Heaven. This new creation fulfills God's promises to God's people. Friends, these are some of the most comforting words found in all Scripture. This is a passage that you can go back to time and time again, as many times as needed, to be reminded that God's presence will comfort us and protect us from the pain and death of the things that have passed away.

Both of these people had to deal with a lot before they got back on their feet. But more so than anything, despite the pain and suffering they endured, they continued to care for other people, and other people showed that they cared for them. This is an example of discipleship in action, maybe without even realizing it. John 13:31-35 says, *"31 So, when he had gone out, Jesus said, "Now the Son of Man is glorified, and God is glorified in Him. 32 If God is glorified in Him, God will also glorify Him in Himself, and glorify Him immediately. 33 Little children, I shall be with you a little while longer. You will seek Me; and as I said to the Jews, 'Where I am going, you cannot come,' so now I say to you. 34 A new commandment I give to you, that you love one another; as I have loved you, that you also love one another. 35 By this all will know that you are My disciples, if you have love for one another."*

Jesus has tried to prepare us to live without him in physical presence among us. With that, Jesus understood that sometimes our faith might waiver a bit. And even with damaged faith, God's grace and mercy still heals us. The woman ended up getting back on her feet about seven years after her husband's death. She was blessed with a new job, a new home, and a new husband who takes pretty good care of her. The man, after battling with his insurance company for about eight months, was able to have a new home built, had new furniture and household items donated to him, and his family continues to live out their lives as if nothing had happened. Both the man and the woman in these stories profess a belief in God's healing power that got them through it. God's promises are always fulfilled. His promises to me, and His promises to you.

Did you drive anywhere today? Did you ride in a car a passenger today? You had confidence in the driving abilities of someone, if so. You had confidence in the vehicle you were in. If you are currently indoors, you have confidence that the roof isn't about to cave in on top of you. I know, it seems abstract at the moment. Just follow along.

A while back I rode down to Austin with my Chief Deputy to challenge the state exam to be certified experts in Civil Process. This is the highest level of certification in this field that the state offers and the test is notoriously one of the hardest. We were pretty confident that we would pass. After all, he and I worked in this specialized field more than rest of our office, we're both certified instructors in this field, and we'd been studying for the past nine weeks. So our scheduled time arrived and we walked into the satellite office of Texas State University who administers the testing. We were told to sit and wait in the lobby until they called us back. I felt pretty good about it, I knew I was going to breeze through it. We had practically memorized the hundred-plus page study guide. We're finally called back by one of the administrators who put us in separate rooms and took up our cell phones. She lays the test on the table in front of me, hands me a pencil, and tells me I have 60 minutes to finish. She walked out and closed the door. I'm sitting there like a racecar driver, revving my engine. I'm completely stoked, I think I'm going to knock this out quick!

Question #1...yep, that's an easy question...

Question #2...even easier than the first one...

I get down to question #5 and not only do I not know the answer, I have trouble just reading the wording in the question. Next question-same situation. All the sudden my confidence begins to fail me and I realize, "Uh oh, these questions weren't in the study guide." I start thinking how bad it would be for the county to have spent hundreds of dollars on me to come all the way down to Austin, pay my travel expenses, pay for my hotel, pay for this exam...and then I fail it. Forty minutes later I've answered all the questions to the best of my ability and I turn in exam for grading. The Chief Deputy and I sit patiently in the lobby while they grade the tests. My nerves are shot and I don't feel too good about the results. I'm finally called back into the administrator's office and guess what—I passed with flying colors.

It was a roller-coaster of confidence. I started out overly-confident in my abilities, then I didn't have much confidence at all. Confidence is something we all invest in. We have confidence in ourselves. We are reluctant to do things we are not good at or familiar with, but have no problem doing things we do well. We have confidence in others. You wouldn't get in the car with someone that you didn't think could drive. If you were an employer you wouldn't hire someone you didn't think could do the job.

While this type of confidence is confidence in the flesh, what *spiritual confidence* do we put into Christ?

Philippians 3:4-14.

3:4 though I also might have confidence in the flesh. If anyone else thinks he may have confidence in the flesh, I more so: 5 circumcised the eighth day, of the stock of Israel, of the tribe of Benjamin, a Hebrew of the Hebrews;

concerning the law, a Pharisee; 6 concerning zeal, persecuting the church; concerning the righteousness which is in the law, blameless.

7 But what things were gain to me, these I have counted loss for Christ. 8 Yet indeed I also count all things loss for the excellence of the knowledge of Christ Jesus my Lord, for whom I have suffered the loss of all things, and count them as rubbish, that I may gain Christ 9 and be found in Him, not having my own righteousness, which is from the law, but that which is through faith in Christ, the righteousness which is from God by faith; 10 that I may know Him and the power of His resurrection, and the fellowship of His sufferings, being conformed to His death, 11 if, by any means, I may attain to the resurrection from the dead.

12 Not that I have already attained, or am already perfected; but I press on, that I may lay hold of that for which Christ Jesus has also laid hold of me. 13 Brethren, I do not count myself to have apprehended; but one thing I do, forgetting those things which are behind and reaching forward to those things which are ahead, 14 I press toward the goal for the prize of the upward call of God in Christ Jesus.

What in the world is Paul trying to say here? This is a fairly confusing piece of Scripture, so let me sum it up. Paul is telling the church in Philippi that he used to be completely confident in himself, that he made his success, but now puts all his confidence in Jesus Christ. Now this might not seem all that different from other Bible verses, but Paul actually wrote this while he was chained to a wall in a Roman prison. How remarkable is it that despite his current state of being, he still expresses joy, hope, and confidence in Christ.

Spiritual confidence is different than faith. Faith is something we decide to have and stick to even when we don't have concrete evidence. Confidence is trust through experience—trusting God because God has proven to be trustworthy. God is driving the car, you're climbing in the passenger seat and you're not afraid because you've ridden with God before and you know he can drive. Spiritual confidence is having experiences with Christ, and trusting Christ for the future. Unlike my experience with the confidence roller-coaster with the exam, the confidence we can find in Christ is perfectly steady.

Resurrection of the body: when the body is dead, it is through Christ that it will be resurrected. When the body of Christ (the church) becomes dead, it is through Christ that it will be resurrected. Resurrection requires confidence in Jesus Christ. When the body is dead, it cannot do anything. But we are confident that Christ will bring life back to that body. When faced with things that we cannot overcome by ourselves, we should remain confident in Christ. A time will come where this ministry, this church, every person will be in a state of dying, and it's at that time that we must have complete and total confidence in our Lord and Savior Jesus Christ...our resurrection.

E arly in my ministry as I began studies in theology, I made a startling observation. At least, it was startling to me. It was the observation that so many people seemed to believe that they knew what their afterlife would entail. The majority of Christians I know believed, beyond a doubt, that they were going to heaven when they leave this mortal life. Some, most whom I knew to be good people, were convinced that they were going to Hell because of something they had done or continued to do. But the truth is that we, as human beings, cannot make this judgement for ourselves. Scripture has given us an instruction manual to give us a better quality of life-and afterlife. But the final judgement has been and always will be up to God.

Since we tend to believe that we know how God thinks and feels about us and our actions, we often punish ourselves and others here in this life. While we know the season of Lent is a test of our will-power for God and a time of spiritual preparation, it is also a time to be repentant of that which burdens us.

Luke 13:1-9.

13:1 At that very time there were some present who told him about the Galileans whose blood Pilate had mingled with their sacrifices. 2 He asked them, "Do you think that because these Galileans suffered in this way they were worse sinners than all other Galileans? 3 No, I tell you; but unless you repent, you will all perish as they did. 4 Or those eighteen who were killed when the tower of Siloam fell on them—do you think that they were worse offenders than all the others living in Jerusalem? 5 No, I tell you; but unless you repent, you will all perish just as they did."

6 Then he told this parable: "A man had a fig tree planted in his vineyard; and he came looking for fruit on it and found none. 7 So he said to the gardener, 'See here! For three years I have come looking for fruit on this fig tree, and still I find none. Cut it down! Why should it be wasting the soil?' 8 He replied, 'Sir, let it alone for one more year, until I dig around it and put manure on it. 9 If it bears fruit next year, well and good; but if not, you can cut it down.'"

One of my favorite things about the gospel is that Jesus doesn't sugar-coat or downplay anything. He tells it like it is, and in this day and age I think that's something we can all appreciate.

Jesus is posed with the question, "Is so-and-so's sin greater than those people's sin?"

And Jesus' reply is, "No, and you better stop worrying about other people's sin and worry about yourself!" And we do that by being repentant.

So admittedly it took me awhile to understand what this meant. I used to think that this simply meant that I had to confess my sins to God, be sorry about it, and ask for forgiveness, and that the end result, if done correctly would result in my afterlife being spent in Heaven. I've learned that all that's somewhat true, but misses the mark for the most part, and our Scripture today helps explain what is meant.

First, notice that at no point does Jesus condemn anyone to Hell. He says if they don't repent they'll perish. Die. Cease to live. Now, I can think of many people I know

112

who are alive, but cease to live. Most of us probably know someone like that. Perhaps they are spiritually dead. Perhaps it's an emotional death. Perhaps it's a relationship that will perish. Every married man knows about repentance in marriages. Or, at least he should.

The second point in our text is that we become so focused on the future in some far off, distant version of Heaven that we forget that we, in fact, live presently in the Kingdom of God. The Kingdom of God, also called the Kingdom of Heaven, is defined as 'the fulfillment on Earth of God's will.' This is the spiritual realm in which God reigns. I have news for you, you're sitting in it right now. We can experience great, amazing things with God right here, right now. We can also create our own 'Hell on Earth' within that same spiritual realm.

A while back I received a phone call from a woman I had known for many years. She said she needed desperately to talk to me face to face. I drove out to her home and she met me in the driveway. She looked like she hadn't slept in a long time, and I could tell she'd lost weight.

She said, "Thanks for coming. I really needed someone to talk to." She went on to tell me that she was having trouble eating and sleeping. She'd been abusing prescription medication. She had nearly completely isolated herself. I asked her why she was in the state she was in. She went on to tell me that a couple months prior she'd struck a young man on a bicycle with her car and left him on the side of the road where he died. She fled the scene and the guilt was eating her alive. While this was under extreme circumstances, a common result of such guilt or personal responsibility causes similar issues. In such situations we don't have to be condemned to Hell for punishment, we're already living it here on Earth.

Things eat away at our soul. We become mentally, physically, emotionally, and spiritually crippled. Repentance doesn't just mean that we confess and ask forgiveness. It also means *we* forgive others. Whether we have to forgive someone else for something they've done, or if we have to forgive ourselves, forgiveness is required. God forgives His children, but his children are far less forgiving. Thus, we condemn ourselves with judgements we're not meant to make. And when we do that, we often fail to live as Christian disciples, we fail to maintain a balance of faith and good works.

In Jesus' parable, he tells a story of a barren fig tree. Now, imagine you're the fig tree.

The owner of this vineyard tells the gardener, "Hey, this fig tree doesn't produce any fruit. It's taking up space, let's dig it up so we can replace it with a better fig tree."

But the gardener bargains with the owner and says, "Hey, give me a little bit of time to nurture this tree. If it still doesn't produce fruit, we'll get rid of it." Aren't you glad that there's a gardener there to nurture and encourage you? Friends, that gardener is Christ. And Christ will nurture us in all the ways that he can...through prayer, through scripture, through mission...however He can.

Lent is a season of spiritual preparation, and part of preparation is going cleaning our slate of whatever might be cluttering it up.

"What I Am"

Colossians 1:1-14:

1:1 Paul, an apostle of Christ Jesus by the will of God, and Timothy our brother,

2 To God's holy people in Colossae, the faithful brothers and sisters in Christ:

Grace and peace to you from God our Father.

3 We always thank God, the Father of our Lord Jesus Christ, when we pray for you, 4 because we have heard of your faith in Christ Jesus and of the love you have for all God's people— 5 the faith and love that spring from the hope stored up for you in heaven and about which you have already heard in the true message of the gospel 6 that has come to you. In the same way, the gospel is bearing fruit and growing throughout the whole world—just as it has been doing among you since the day you heard it and truly understood God's grace. 7 You learned it from Epaphras, our dear fellow servant, who is a faithful minister of Christ on our behalf, 8 and who also told us of your love in the Spirit.

9 For this reason, since the day we heard about you, we have not stopped praying for you. We continually ask God to fill you with the knowledge of his will through all the wisdom and understanding that the Spirit gives, 10 so that you may live a life worthy of the Lord and please him in every way: bearing fruit in every good work, growing in the knowledge of God, 11 being strengthened with all power according to his glorious might so that you may have great endurance and patience, 12 and giving joyful thanks to the

Father, who has qualified you to share in the inheritance of his holy people in the kingdom of light. 13 For he has rescued us from the dominion of darkness and brought us into the kingdom of the Son he loves, 14 in whom we have redemption, the forgiveness of sins.

The Apostle Paul was always one of my favorite figures in biblical history. He fashioned his ministry around not only making Christian disciples, but coaching the early Christian churches to help them better understand the theology and grow their faith. Each of Paul's Epistles is evidence of this. One of the recurring messages that Paul presents to his audience, including in our text today, is that "we have inherited the power of God to be His church." This means that rather than being reactive to things that God does around us, we have the power to be proactive, bringing God into our daily lives.

A great example of this is the power of "*I am.*" When we begin a sentence with the words, "I am…," the words that follow to make up the rest of the sentence are often willed into fruition. Also, the words that follow often reflect what we believe to be the truth. I recall one day I was counseling a man who'd been struggling with some bad choices he'd previously made in life. He'd spent some time in jail, been through a couple divorces, and had most recently lost his job.

I remember asking him what he felt that he needed to get back on track and he replied, "I am worthless, it doesn't make a difference." Friends, the words that follow "I am" are some of the most important words you will speak in the course of any given day. This man had little hope with his current state. As long as he believed he was worthless, he had no reason to strive for a better life. When he said he was worthless he was really saying, "There's no point in trying, I'm not going to get better. I've given up."

The power of "I am" is more effective than we often credit. God has given us this power as a form of self-maintenance. Imagine a car that could change its own oil. The engine creates the energy that puts the car in motion, but the oil keeps the engine running. After a while that oil gets burned and becomes less effective, so it has to be changed out for some fresh oil. If the oil isn't changed, the engine eventually stops working. As disciples we hope to make positive changes in the world. Before we can do that, we have to at least be able to make positive changes for ourselves.

A person might say "I am always tired."

Instead, they might say, "I am going to try to get more rest so I can perform better tomorrow."

A person might say "I am too old to do much anymore."

Instead, they might say, "I am experienced and a great deal of wisdom to share with the world."

Or a person might say, "I am worthless."

Instead, they might say, "I am going to make a better life for myself."

An important thing that we all should remember is that God is not the only force at work in the world. So often we fail to respect the influence that evil has on us. Satan often uses two methods to do this. One is be leading us to believe that he does not exist. The other is by deceiving us in ways that lead us away from God. Quite often, he uses both of these tactics in the words following, "I am..." It's subtle, it's easy to miss, but it happens to all of us fairly frequently. When this happens, we need to change our oil. We have the God-given power to change those lies we let ourselves believe into positive truths.

My daughter was my first-born biological child. I was nineteen years old when she was born. I remember being in the delivery room and the doctor asked me to cut the umbilical cord. She handed me these forceps and I was shaking so hard that I almost couldn't do it. The first time I held her I was full of emotions, I had no idea how to be a dad. I was convinced that I wasn't going to be a good parent.

I remember saying, "I am not cut out for parenthood." Let me tell you, for the sake of all my children, I had to change that "I am."

Yes, friends, God has given us many powers for us to use in our ministry. These powers serve as a guiding light for some, as a shield from evil, a source of strength at times. Never underestimate the power of "I am."

"Plenty of Time"

Luke 10:38-42:

10:38 Now it happened as they went that He entered a certain village; and a certain woman named Martha welcomed Him into her house. 39 And she had a sister called Mary, who also sat at Jesus' feet and heard His word. 40 But Martha was distracted with much serving, and she approached Him and said, "Lord, do You not care that my sister has left me to serve alone? Therefore tell her to help me."

41 And Jesus answered and said to her, "Martha, Martha, you are worried and troubled about many things. 42 But one thing is needed, and Mary has chosen that good part, which will not be taken away from her."

Time management: it's not something that is particularly talked about in a lot of Sunday sermons. As long as we make time for God then we're good, right? Well, that's probably not as right as we'd expect. The fact of the matter is that we live our lives in measurements of time. Minute by minute, hour by hour, day by day, we work, we eat food, we maintain relationships. We're always doing something. The problem is that while we live our lives in these increments of time, God does not. God is God all the time, doing things in our lives all the time, and yet we often reserve a portion of our time to God.

Remember, the Devil uses two primary tactics to influence us: leading us to believe that he does not exist, and through deception. One of the greatest deceptions is that we have plenty of time.

My grandfather and I were particularly close. The problem was that he was a thousand miles in Pennsylvania and I was here in Texas. As far as I know, Grandpa never once turned on a computer, and he certainly never sent emails. Our correspondence was done the old-fashioned way with a pen and paper. For most of my childhood and adolescence he would write to me every couple of months, and I would always write back. This continued until my early 20's. I was working on starting a family, beginning a career, buying my first house—I was busy doing what I thought were important things. I would receive letters in the mail, and I always loved hearing from him. But instead of sitting down and writing him back right away, I'd put it off for a few days, a week, a month. Eventually I got to the point where I stopped responding. I figured that once I had my life situated the way I wanted it, I would have plenty of time to write letters to Grandpa. But then he was gone. No more letters, no more chances to tell him about the things I wanted to tell him about. I thought I had more time.

In 2018 when my step-mother got sick with cancer, I started to experience this again. I thought I'd have more time on this earth with her. I'd learned my lesson though. I made it a point to spend as much time as possible with her before her passing. I didn't wait around. Friends, every moment, God is sending you letters hoping for a reply. How busy are we?

C.S. Lewis taught that your life was a continuum. On one end was wholeness, and on the other end was destruction. Every time you make a decision, that decision takes you either a step towards God, or a step towards destruction. When we take on too much, when we are distracted with everything that we have going on, it can be hard to tell which way we're headed.

American pastor Kevin DeYoung identified three significant dangers of being too busy in his book titled *"Crazy Busy."*

One is that busyness can ruin our joy. As Christians our lives are meant to be marked by joy, according to Philippians 4:4. If we're so caught up in our daily activities that we have no joy left in us when we get home, we're too busy.

The second is that busyness can choke out our spiritual hearts. While there's some folks who have left their faith as a result of some traumatic or unpleasant experience, pew surveys have shown that the majority of people who cease taking part in church activities do so as a result of having conflicting schedules. It's all the worries of a crazy busy life that chokes out our spiritualism.

The third is possibly the most dangerous. Busyness can cover up the rot in our souls. Have you ever heard someone when they're dealing with a stressful situation say, "I'm trying to stay busy so I won't think about it." While this can be a constructive approach on a short term basis, people who do this as a long-term solution to serious problems are failing to deal with something more serious. The end result to this is almost always our own destruction.

Remember friends, we are not perfect, but we do serve a perfect God. Don't let yourself get over encumbered with the daily hustle of life. Take time to think about where each is decision is leading you. Take time to find that joy that's supposed to mark the lives of Christians. Take time to be present with God.

"On My Own?"

Luke 11:1-13:

11:1 Now it came to pass, as He was praying in a certain place, when He ceased, that one of His disciples said to Him, "Lord, teach us to pray, as John also taught his disciples."

2 So He said to them, "When you pray, say:

Our Father in heaven,

Hallowed be Your name.

Your kingdom come.

Your will be done

On earth as it is in heaven.

3 Give us day by day our daily bread.

4 And forgive us our sins,

For we also forgive everyone who is indebted to us.

And do not lead us into temptation,

But deliver us from the evil one."

A Friend Comes at Midnight

5 And He said to them, "Which of you shall have a friend, and go to him at midnight and say to him, 'Friend, lend me three loaves; 6 for a friend of mine has come to me on his journey, and I have nothing to set before him'; 7 and he will answer from within and say, 'Do not trouble me; the door is now shut, and my children are with me in bed; I cannot rise and give to you'? 8 I say to you, though he will not rise and give to him because he is his friend, yet because of his persistence he will rise and give him as many as he needs.

9 "So I say to you, ask, and it will be given to you; seek, and you will find; knock, and it will be opened to you. 10 For everyone who asks receives, and he who seeks finds, and to him who knocks it will be opened. 11 If a son asks for bread from any father among you, will he give him a stone? Or if he asks for a fish, will he give him a serpent instead of a fish? 12 Or if he asks for an egg, will he offer him a scorpion? 13 If you then, being evil, know how to give good gifts to your children, how much more will your heavenly Father give the Holy Spirit to those who ask Him!"

As summer break comes to a close, teachers and kids and parents are getting geared up for the start of a new school year. I'm a busy guy, I can barely remember what I did when I got up this morning, but I can remember my first several days at school. Isn't it weird how you can recall certain things? My mom took a picture of me with the old Polaroid camera that morning of my first day in kindergarten. I was wearing a pair of red and blue shorts that she had made me and I had the dorkiest haircut you'd ever seen (this was in the mid-1980's). I remember her walking me into the school, down the hall to Mrs. Wisdom's room. I remember the way that classroom smelled. If "unfamiliar" was an odor, that's what it smelled like. When my mom hugged me goodbye, I remember a certain sense of panic. Here I am in an unfamiliar place, with a bunch of unfamiliar kids, and to be honest, it was scary as hell. Tears started to well up in my eyes, and Mrs. Wisdom must've noticed. It was at that time that this gentle, calm, old woman took me by the hand

and assured me that everything's okay and she'll show me all around. After a couple days of having that assurance and guidance, I knew my way around the school, I knew the rules, and now I was excited to come to school! I was a big kid now!

Although as Christians we would like to believe that God holds our hand and tells us exactly what to do and when, that just simply isn't the case. The truth is that we begin like infants. When we are born our mothers nurture us and feed us and do everything for us. But as we grow a bit mom stops holding us all the time. We're expected to start doing some things for ourselves. We become more independent. But nevertheless, children need their mothers to fall back on, to guide them, and protect them. It's a lot like it was in those first days of school. Mom wasn't there to hold my hand through it all. I had to learn how to be a student. And when I didn't know what to do, Mrs. Wisdom was right there ready to help me.

Friends, God has given us the power of self-reliance. While this might sound like something that separates us from God, it's actually the complete opposite. You see, as we grow in our faith, our spiritual maturity, if you will, we naturally become more independent. Imagine that kindergartener now during the last day of school. He knows the routine, he knows the layout of the school, he knows the rules. But when he's faced with something he's unsure of, he knows he can turn to his teacher for guidance.

Christ is our teacher. Christ has been our teacher for two thousand years. Making decisions requires a great deal of independence, but knowing where to find guidance is the key wise decisions. Marriage, home buying, career choices, college—you can decide on your own that you want to do these things, but you'd better have a teacher to guide you when you run into the unfamiliar. Your church family, your pastor, your mentors, and, of course, your Savior Christ Himself are all there to help you on your journey.

Have you ever been in a car wreck? Have you ever been so sick or sustained an injury of some type that was so bad you had to go to the hospital? Have you ever seen a house on fire? Think about what these situations had in common: they needed immediate attention, right? Why? Because you're hurt, afraid, in danger, maybe other people are in danger. Remember how you felt in those situations. Let's call those feelings "infirmity." Infirmity is when we are in a physically or mentally weakened state.

Now, imagine being in one of those situations and calling for help, but we're told we'll have to wait until tomorrow. Bizarre as it might seem, such was a reality in Jesus' time.

Luke 13:10-17:

13:10 Now he was teaching in one of the synagogues on the sabbath. 11 And just then there appeared a woman with a spirit that had crippled her for eighteen years. She was bent over and was quite unable to stand up straight. 12 When Jesus saw her, he called her over and said, "Woman, you are set free from your ailment." 13 When he laid his hands on her, immediately she stood up straight and began praising God. 14 But the leader of the synagogue, indignant because Jesus had cured on the sabbath, kept saying to the crowd, "There are six days on which work ought to be done; come on those days and be cured, and not on the sabbath day." 15 But the Lord answered him and said, "You hypocrites! Does not each of you on the sabbath untie his ox or his donkey from the manger, and lead it away to give it water? 16 And ought not this woman, a daughter of Abraham whom Satan bound for eighteen

126

long years, be set free from this bondage on the sabbath day?" 17 When he said this, all his opponents were put to shame; and the entire crowd was rejoicing at all the wonderful things that he was doing.

I don't mention my father's side of the family tree all that much in my sermons. The truth of the matter is that I've only started learning about my paternal ancestors over the past decade or so. My grandfather on my father's side was born in Philadelphia, Pennsylvania. I got to meet him before he passed away in 2013. He was a strong man who liked his brandy and cigars. He was one of the first in his family to be born in the United States. His father, my great-grandfather, Pasquale Lerro, and his wife, Justina, were from Campania, a town outside Naples, Italy. So, the year is 1896 and Italy has just begun the Italo-Ethiopian War, which was an expensive and bloody attempt to conquer Ethiopia. Thousands and thousands of Italians are killed, wounded, and taken prisoner. Italy, which is already suffering from rampant poverty, becomes even more financially crippled from the war. Rioting and strife break out across Italy. It is at that time that Pasquale and Justina marry each other and board a ship destined for Philadelphia. According to immigration records, they were twelve years old when they immigrated to the United States and began a new life.

Now, many of you find that hard to comprehend: getting married at twelve years old, starting a family, and making a living. The truth of the matter is that the traditional marrying age in 1896 Italy, even back in Jesus' day, was twelve to twenty years of age. One of the biggest reasons why this tradition existed is because of a short life expectancy, which for men and women both averaged thirty-eight to forty-two years. When you look at it in those terms, it doesn't seem so bizarre.

Traditions, to some degree, have a life expectancy of their own. Due to changes such as modern medicine, diet, and environment, people live longer these days. We no longer need to hurry up and get hitched at such an early age.

In our text, we hear of Jesus healing a crippled woman. He releases her from her infirmity, but just as he does so, the leader of the synagogue attempts to admonish Jesus because He's working on the Sabbath, which the Jewish call *Shabbat*. Never mind the fact that He's performing a miracle. Never mind the fact that He's helping someone in need. The only thing this priest focuses on is that fact that Christ, in his eyes, is breaking one of God's commandments: remember the Sabbath and keep it holy, as well as Jewish religious law. The Jewish tradition of paying homage to God on the Sabbath consisted of practically nothing that resembled work. While we are used to the Sabbath being on Sunday, Jewish tradition observes it from Friday night until an hour after sundown on Saturday. During that period of time work was prohibited. Saturday's meals were prepared on Friday. Medicine could not be administered on Shabbat. Such was Jewish religious law. But Jesus, seeing the need to break tradition, did so. It's not that Jesus forgot tradition, or disrespected it, He merely applied logic to an antiquated practice when it became necessary. God had applied grace to the equation.

As much as we like the comfort of tradition, Christians must be able to adapt to changing times, perhaps even creating new traditions. A favorite quote of nearly every dying church is, "we've always done it that way." The same is true for us. While observing tradition is fine, we as disciples must be willing to adapt to modern world concerns and infirmities, and trust God's grace to see us through such times. Possibly the most important thing we can do as disciples is share God's love with anyone, at any time, under any circumstances.

My faith has gotten me through some tough times. But, you know, in the midst of a crisis or something significant, it's sometimes hard to think about how God factors into the equation. The world can be a chaotic, messed up place. People are always fighting with each other. People do some really awful stuff to one another. Likewise, people do some really awful stuff to themselves. Let me tell you something, I'm about sick and tired of hearing about mass shootings. Every time I turn on the news or social media, it seems like there's been another shooting. Here's the scary part: twenty-five years ago we'd hear about a mass shooting and we'd be shocked, but now it's almost expected. I don't know about you, but I literally sit and wonder when and where the next one will happen. In fact, it's so common now, law enforcement around the world have specialized training in "active shooter" scenarios. We call this training A.L.E.R.R.T., which is an acronym for Advanced Law Enforcement Rapid Response Training. One of the things taught is, in fact, to be alert. We call this being vigilant. We even have "active shooter" training for civilians in the workplace, as well as for school faculty and churches. Again, one of the first things taught is to be vigilant.

In El Paso, a gunman walked into a crowded marketplace carrying a rifle. It's reported that there were dozens and dozens of people in that marketplace. The gunman walks across the parking lot and unleashes his evil as he enters a Walmart. Before he was apprehended, he claimed twenty-two lives and wounded nearly thirty others.

Yet, none of those dozens of people saw him coming. None of them knew his intentions. None of them were able to stop him until it was too late.

If we are going to make it, we have to be alert. Let me ask you this: Are you alert? Are you spiritually alert?

Luke 12:32-40:

12:32 "Do not be afraid, little flock, for it is your Father's good pleasure to give you the kingdom. 33 Sell your possessions, and give alms. Make purses for yourselves that do not wear out, an unfailing treasure in heaven, where no thief comes near and no moth destroys. 34 For where your treasure is, there your heart will be also.

35 "Be dressed for action and have your lamps lit; 36 be like those who are waiting for their master to return from the wedding banquet, so that they may open the door for him as soon as he comes and knocks. 37 Blessed are those slaves whom the master finds alert when he comes; truly I tell you, he will fasten his belt and have them sit down to eat, and he will come and serve them. 38 If he comes during the middle of the night, or near dawn, and finds them so, blessed are those slaves.

39 "But know this: if the owner of the house had known at what hour the thief was coming, he would not have let his house be broken into. 40 You also must be ready, for the Son of Man is coming at an unexpected hour."

Friends, remaining alert means we have to filter out the distractions. It's disgusting when politicians and the media tell us the problem is this and that, and they tell us how we're supposed to feel about it. Evil is at work in the world. We can ban every gun, or we can arm every citizen.

Mental illness, racism...the only thing we need to worry about is that evil is at work, and evil doesn't need guns, it doesn't need politicians, it doesn't need an agenda. It only needs weak faith.

Are you spiritually alert?

Have you seen any of those Avengers or Justice League movies? Have you ever seen Batman? You know, when I was a kid, we didn't see them in movies, we read their comic books. I was particularly fascinated with X-Men. I think X-Men was my favorite. One thing I always liked about those superheroes is the fact that you were usually always able to tell who the good guys were. They characterized everything you'd expect in a superhero: they were the embodiment of justice. They helped rescue the oppressed, or heal the sick, or help people in need by defeating some form of evil. And they did so by being always alert. Sound familiar?

In a world of chaos and evil, we can rest assured that there is someone who is able to defeat evil, who is able to rescue the oppressed, care for the sick...do all the good that needs to be done. That superhero is none other than..............*you*. God has given us these powers by giving us His Son, Jesus Christ. And only through the love of Christ will evil be defeated. But we can't defeat evil if we're distracted.

ARE YOU SPIRITUALLY ALERT?

E very Sunday morning, all around the world, millions of Christian disciples woke up and got ready for church. While you were doing this, even more millions of people of people did not. Even people who believe in Christ woke up and, for one reason or another, did not go to church. They did not leave their home and share the message with anyone. They did not go out and help a stranger. They woke up and embraced some kind of excuse as to why they wouldn't follow Christ this morning. "I don't feel like it. I have too much to do at home. I can serve God in my own way, on my own schedule."

Years ago I worked part time as a substitute school teacher. Most of the time when I was called in to cover I was assigned to a kindergarten classroom. Now, I've been a marine and a cop, but that was one of the most challenging jobs I'd ever had. I never appreciated my own children until I had to take care of other people's. If I was reading to them, they were okay. But getting them to do things was like pulling teeth. I would give them instructions, and they'd find any excuse to not follow them. Yeah, those were fun times.

Jesus' message to His disciples was simple. "Follow me." It sounds easy enough to do, but why do we still manage to struggle with following His instructions? Let's try an exercise. I'm going to give you some simple instructions. For each of the following statements I have written, say to yourself, "Follow me!" Got it? Okay.

-I'm too tired to go to church.

-It's my only day off.

-I'm not comfortable in church.

-I don't know that much about the Bible.

-I don't have good clothes to wear to church.

-Let's step it up a bit.

-I'm a forgiving person, but I just can't get over what he did to me.

-I'm a Christian, but I don't agree with certain types of people.

-I can serve God in my own way, without a church.

-I'm too much of a sinner, I've done too many bad things.

-I can't make that big of a difference in the world.

Friends, Jesus has heard every excuse that has ever been thought up. People have made excuse after excuse to keep themselves separated from the love of Jesus Christ. I used to be one of these people. In fact, there was a point in time where I said every one of those things myself. Jesus has had to deal with people on their own program since the beginning of His ministry, which wasn't always popular with the locals. In the Gospel of Luke Jesus travels to the village of the Samaritans with several of His disciples. Now, we've grown accustomed to Samaritans as being "good." That wasn't always the case. You see, Samaritans and Jews were not friends. Samaritans were not Jewish, they practiced Samaritanism. They believed that their version of the Holy Torah was the pure and original version, and that the Jewish version was a corrupted version. They did not particularly like Jews. And they did not like Jesus. Before Jesus made it to the Samaritan village, He sent out messengers to prepare a place for Him there, but they were not turned away because they were Jews. So the group travels on down the road with Jesus. And as they go people keep approaching Jesus wanting to support His ministry.

Luke 9:57-62:

9:57 As they were going along the road, someone said to him, "I will follow you wherever you go." 58 And Jesus said to him, "Foxes have holes, and birds of the air have nests; but the Son of Man has nowhere to lay his head." 59 To another he said, "Follow me." But he said, "Lord, first let me go and bury my father." 60 But Jesus said to him, "Let the dead bury their own dead; but as for you, go and proclaim the kingdom of God." 61 Another said, "I will follow you, Lord; but let me first say farewell to those at my home." 62 Jesus said to him, "No one who puts a hand to the plow and looks back is fit for the kingdom of God."

There's a lot of good sermon material in that single passage, but the bottom line is this: God has called us to be His church, it's time that we stop making excuses. At the end of the day, we can reflect on what we accomplished. Did I make enough money? Did I get enough housework done? Did I spend enough time with the people I wanted to spend time with? The most important question we can ask ourselves is, "Did I serve God?"

Each one of us is a minister of Christ's church and each of us is someone's picture of Christianity. Each of us has a call to mission. Jesus tells us how to do this. It's two simple words: "Follow me."

I keep my car keys in the top right drawer of my dresser, that's where they go. Every time I come home, they go in that drawer. The other day I was running behind schedule and was about to be late. I rush out the door, get to the car, and guess what: I can't find my car keys. Being sure that I had not deviated from my morning routine of grabbing my keys on my way out, I checked all my pockets. Not there. I retraced my steps, looking at the kitchen counter top, kitchen table, the bathroom counter, everywhere I could think I'd been where I might have inadvertently set them down. Not there. Panic and frustration began to set in, my blood pressure shot up. You'll never guess where I found them: the dresser drawer, right where they were supposed to be. Not only that, but in the drawer next to my keys was my wallet, which I evidently didn't have.

Have you ever searched for something only to find it exactly where it's supposed to be? Mary and Joseph did.

Luke 2:41-52.

2:41 Now every year his parents went to Jerusalem for the festival of the Passover. 42 And when he was twelve years old, they went up as usual for the festival. 43 When the festival was ended and they started to return, the boy Jesus stayed behind in Jerusalem, but his parents did not know it. 44 Assuming that he was in the group of travelers, they went a day's journey. Then they started to look for him among their relatives and friends. 45 When they did not find him, they returned to Jerusalem to search for him. 46 After three days they found him in the temple, sitting among the teachers, listening to them and asking them questions. 47 And all who heard him were amazed at his understanding and his answers. 48 When his parents saw him they were astonished; and his mother said to him, "Child, why have you treated us like this? Look, your father and I have been searching for you in great anxiety." 49 He said to them, "Why were you searching for me? Did you not know that I must be in my Father's house?" 50 But they did not understand what he said to them. 51 Then he went down with them and came to Nazareth, and was obedient to them. His mother treasured all these things in her heart.

52 And Jesus increased in wisdom and in years, and in divine and human favor.

According to the law, Jewish males were required to visit Jerusalem three times a year. Jesus' parents are pious Jews and they're visiting Jerusalem for the feast of the Passover. The trip from Nazareth to Jerusalem is about sixty miles, so this journey is always somewhat of a big deal with required planning and preparation. In Jewish culture, when boy turns twelve years old he is considered to be a man, at least in regards to religious duties. So Jesus, who's now twelve years old and being aware of his faith traditions, sets out with his parents and other relatives for the trip to Jerusalem for the Passover, which lasts 7 days. They get there, they celebrate for a few days, now it's time to go home. Joseph and Mary and their friends and family, travel a whole day, and then realize, "Hey, we don't have Jesus!"

So after traveling for a day, spending another day traveling back to Jerusalem, and a third day searching for Jesus, where do they find him? In the temple, sitting not before the teachers, but among them. And Jesus is asking them questions about faith. Yes, even though we're told

Jesus had amazing answers, he still had things to learn. Look at that last verse: "And Jesus increased in wisdom and in years...."

Well how about that? Even Jesus Christ had things to learn, and the older he got the more wisdom he had.

Joseph and Mary spent three days searching for Jesus. They end up finding him in church. Imagine that. How many people are searching for something everywhere except where they should be looking?

Think about this: According to research 69% of Americans currently identify themselves as being Christians.

This is down from 85% in 1990, 81% in 2001, and 78%in 2012. Professions of belief in Christ are declining.

Now, remembering that 69% of America claims to be Christian, the same study shows that only 37% of Christians attend church. This number has also declined over the years.

Fifty years ago you didn't have to ask someone if they went to church, you asked where they went to church. Sadly, nowadays, the question isn't even about church attendance, it's about whether someone even believes in God.

We have to do a better job at getting in touch with people outside the church. Many, many people are out there looking for the truth. And here we are, looking for disciples to teach as the next generation of Christians. Think about the exact spot where you're sitting right now and ask yourself, "Who's going to be my replacement in this spot when I pass away?"

While there are folks out there who think that the life of the church is the responsibility of the pastor, the truth is that each one of us has a Christian obligation to make disciples. In fact, in the United Methodist Church your pastor is usually only there three to five years before they get sent to another church, but many of the parishioners are there for decades.

We mustn't be afraid of learning new things. That's how we apply what we know about God and grow in our faith. But we also must realize that not everyone is at the same place in their understanding of God. Think of it like this: We're all watching a movie in a movie theatre. But no one saw the very beginning of the movie. Instead, some people came in early in the movie, some came in in the middle of the movie, and some got there really late. While no one saw the whole story from start to finish, everyone working together and sharing their knowledge and understanding of what they know about the story helps piece the story together in a way we can all better understand it.

We have to be willing to learn new things. We have to share and apply what we do know with those who don't know. Before we can make disciples of Christ, we have to *be* disciples of Christ. Let us make a resolution to be open and willing to grow in faith, to start searching for our replacement in the pews, and share our knowledge and understanding with others.

For those of you who are lucky enough to be retired, congratulations. If you're not, your day will come. If you ask me, we all deserve a day off. That's the idea behind Labor Day. Just what is it that we celebrate on Labor Day, anyway? Well, Labor Day is a federal holiday that honors the American labor movement in the 1800's, which still benefits workers today. While you might go in to work thinking you have a terrible job, I assure you, no matter what it is you do (or did) for a living, it was way worse in the nineteenth century when your ancestors were doing it. Working conditions were awful. There were few safety regulations, resulting in horrific work-related injuries and deaths. Immigrants, especially those from Ireland, Italy, and west Europe, blacks and former slaves, Native Americans, and women of any race were paid a significantly lower amount to do the same jobs as men who were born in the U.S. or mainland England. There was no threshold for overtime, companies were loosely regulated when it came to how many hours they could make someone work. Oftentimes, workers were not paid by the hour, but rather by the day or the week. Some employers made their employees work as many twenty hours a day for very low pay, while others who did the exact same job worked an eight hour day. Basically it came down to whether you are male or female, what your race was, and in many places, which side of the Mason-Dixon Line you lived on during the Civil War. The one thing that remained common among all workers: they worked to make companies rich. And let me tell you, capitalism was booming! Factories, steel mills, mines, silos and markets filled with grain, and the food-industry were all expanding. With all this capitalism going on, and workers being treated poorly, the Labor Movement was born. Through solidarity and strong leadership lobbying in Washington, D.C., the wealthy business owners and politicians were forced to acknowledge the importance of the American worker. With the threat of profits being crippled by a strike, conditions were widely improved across-the-board with new laws being put in place. These corporations and politicians had been given a lesson in humility.

Humility was one of Jesus' favorite things to teach about. In the Gospel of Luke we hear about Jesus visiting the house of a leader of the Pharisees. Even in this dangerous venue, Jesus takes the opportunity to change the hearts and minds of others

Luke 14:7-14:

14:7 When he noticed how the guests chose the places of honor, he told them a parable. 8 "When you are invited by someone to a wedding banquet, do not sit down at the place of honor, in case someone more distinguished than you has been invited by your host; 9 and the host who invited both of you may come and say to you, 'Give this person your place,' and then in disgrace you would start to take the lowest place. 10 But when you are invited, go and sit down at the lowest place, so that when your host comes, he may say to you, 'Friend, move up higher'; then you will be honored in the presence of all who sit at the table with you. 11 For all who exalt themselves will be humbled, and those who humble themselves will be exalted."

12 He said also to the one who had invited him, "When you give a luncheon or a dinner, do not invite your friends or your brothers or your relatives or rich neighbors, in case

they may invite you in return, and you would be repaid. 13 But when you give a banquet, invite the poor, the crippled, the lame, and the blind. 14 And you will be blessed, because they cannot repay you, for you will be repaid at the resurrection of the righteous."

It's okay to go to work. It's okay to make money. What's not okay is when we do it for our own personal benefit, and give nothing to others or to God. Are we being the worker, or are we being the greedy corporation? Jesus is clear in His teaching: if we are humble in our offerings to the less fortunate, we will be blessed. But if we only seek to gain for ourselves, God will inevitably humble us.

I'll tell you the story of a man named Colonel Ethan Markham. Markham had been the son of a wealthy investment banker in Boston, Massachusetts in the 1700's. At the dawn of the Revolutionary War, Markham had been pressured to serve in the Continental Army by his family. Having no interest in serving as a foot soldier, Markham used his father's influence to secure himself the rank of Lieutenant. Markham's father assured him that if he achieved greatness and success against the British, he would hand over his company to Ethan at the end of the war. This appealed to Ethan: unimaginable wealth, power, political influence. Markham was willing to risk his life for it. He was given command of a small outfit which fought their way through several battles. Markham was recommended for promotion, and to secure his promotion he assured his commanding officers that they, too, would be rewarded for helping him achieve his success once he took over the company. He eventually obtained the rank of Colonel, now commanding an entire regiment. One evening while on a march through the western woods of New Jersey, Colonel

Markham broke off from the columns with several of his staff to seek lodging in a plantation home about a mile away. After all, he was a Colonel, and Colonels had privileges. Just before sunset, with only a few men riding with him, a shot rang out dropping one of the men's horses. From a nearby tree line, a group of Hessians, German mercenaries working for the British, charged towards them. Out-gunned and outnumbered, Markham gave the command for his men to stand-down. Surrounded, one of the Hessians demanded to know who was in command. You see, the British paid the Hessians well when they killed Americans, but they paid more if they killed American officers. Reluctantly, Markham spoke up. It was in that moment that he realized that all that he had been trying to achieve had been in vain, and was the very thing that was going to cost him his life. If he'd just stayed home, if he'd just been a foot soldier...but he wanted glory for himself, he wanted power and privilege. None of that mattered now. No amount of money, no amount of power or influence. The men were taken prisoner and led to a British encampment. But Colonel Markham was never seen again.

Friends, with humility there's grace, and where there's grace there's God.

"Just Let Go"

One night a young man, we'll call him Michael, was stressed out about issues going on his life. He decides to take a walk to help clear his head. He starts walking down the street and looks up at the sky and he sees a spectacular canvas of stars. The lights near the street are washing out some of the view. He notices a field just up ahead, with no lights around it. Just a nice dark field, perfect for looking at the stars. He walks out into this field, he looks up...the starry sky is amazing. With his gaze fixed on the night sky, he takes a step forward...straight into an old well. Just as he begins to fall, he grabs hold of a tree root that had grown through the bricks. Michael begins to yell for help, but no one can hear him. Michael is terrified. He looks down and sees nothing but empty blackness below. He clings harder. In that moment, all his troubles seemed small and insignificant.

In his despair, he pleads, "God, help me!"

At that moment, Michael hears a voice say, "Just let go." Michael says, "You're crazy! I don't want to die!"

Again, the voice says, "Michael, just let go."

With desperation in his voice and tears in his eyes, Michael clings tighter to root, saying, "Please, God, don't let me die!"

Michael remained in that position, clinging to the root, all night long. When morning broke, Michael is struggling to hang onto this root. Just as the sunlight cut across the horizon, the well becomes visible. Michael was only two feet from the bottom. The well had been dried up and filled in for many years. Michael realized he should have had faith and let go. Someone once told me that story and it's stuck with me ever since.

Hebrews 11:29-12:2:

11:29 By faith the people passed through the Red Sea as if it were dry land, but when the Egyptians attempted to do so they were drowned. 30 By faith the walls of Jericho fell after they had been encircled for seven days. 31 By faith Rahab the prostitute did not perish with those who were disobedient, because she had received the spies in peace.

32 And what more should I say? For time would fail me to tell of Gideon, Barak, Samson, Jephthah, of David and Samuel and the prophets— 33 who through faith conquered kingdoms, administered justice, obtained promises, shut the mouths of lions, 34 quenched raging fire, escaped the edge of the sword, won strength out of weakness, became mighty in war, put foreign armies to flight. 35 Women received their dead by resurrection. Others were tortured, refusing to accept release, in order to obtain a better resurrection. 36 Others suffered mocking and flogging, and even chains and imprisonment. 37 They were stoned to death, they were sawn in two, they were killed by the sword; they went about in skins of sheep and goats, destitute, persecuted, tormented— 38 of whom the world was not worthy. They wandered in deserts and mountains, and in caves and holes in the ground.

39 Yet all these, though they were commended for their faith, did not receive what was promised, 40 since God had provided something better so that they would not, apart from us, be made perfect.

12:1 Therefore, since we are surrounded by so great a cloud of witnesses, let us also lay aside every weight and the sin that clings so closely, and let us run with perseverance the race that is set before us, 2 looking to Jesus the pioneer and perfecter of our faith, who for the sake of the joy that was set before him endured the cross, disregarding its shame, and has taken his seat at the right hand of the throne of God.

Have you ever noticed that when things are going well we often take all the credit? And when things get hard, we begin to lean on our faith more and more, kind of like Michael in our story? The truth is that God is constantly at work in our lives. Right now, I bet some of you are stressed about school starting. Or maybe it's because tomorrow is Monday. You may be thinking, "Oh man, this is going to be hard." Friends, I assure you, all you need is a little faith. God is in it, whatever it is. Don't cling to the root.

My oldest son, Jacob, is in his twenties now. Unlike Mason and Ashlyn (my other children), Jacob struggled with school. High school was particularly difficult. Even though he came to school early for tutorials, math just killed him.

At one point in his fifth year of high school, he said, "Dad, I'm just going to withdraw from school. I'll never pass the math."

I remember telling him, "Son, you'll never accomplish anything if you don't believe you can. Have faith that God will see you through it." Jacob was clinging to the root. It was only when he decided he was going to finish high school no matter what, that he finally let go of that root. He graduated in May 2019.

Friends, if you're holding on to the root, clinging for dear life, let today be the day you let go and put your faith in God.

In the spring of 1992, I remember being squatted down next to the third base line with the rest of the team. Our head coach, Jim, addressed us after our first practice of the new season. For most of us, this would be our last season together before entering high school. Many of us had played on the same team, with the same coaches, since the first grade. However, there were some new kids on the team, guys that had moved into town or whatnot.

Coach Jim said, "This is it. I only need those of you who are here to play baseball. If your priorities are socializing with friends, video games, or anything other than baseball, I won't have much use for you on this team. You might as well not even come to the next practice." Those of us who'd played on Jim's team already knew that for the next several months, baseball owned us. Long practices in the heat, no more junk food after school, and sore muscles. Sometimes when we wanted to go to the lake for a summer outing, we went as a team. In fact, the only things Coach Jim yielded his baseball team to was church and, occasionally, school. Later on in life, I realized that we were a team of champions, not necessarily winners. Well into adulthood I remain friends with the guys who played on that team for all those years. What bonded us was the commitment that we put forth, and all that we shared along the way—the victories, the losses, the injuries, the laughter, and the tears. It turned out that baseball was only the vessel for the things that were truly valuable. That's what Coach Jim wanted us to have. Not trophies.

When Jesus was in the peak of His ministry, people came from all over to see Him and find out what the hype was all about. But here's an interesting fact about Christ: it was never His goal to attract large masses of new disciples. He sought quality over quantity. In fact, throughout the Gospel of Luke, Jesus' words tend to discourage people from following Him, rather than attract their loyalty.

Luke 14:25-33:

14:25 Now large crowds were traveling with him; and he turned and said to them, 26 "Whoever comes to me and does not hate father and mother, wife and children, brothers and sisters, yes, and even life itself, cannot be my disciple. 27 Whoever does not carry the cross and follow me cannot be my disciple. 28 For which of you, intending to build a tower, does not first sit down and estimate the cost, to see whether he has enough to complete it? 29 Otherwise, when he has laid a foundation and is not able to finish, all who see it will begin to ridicule him, 30 saying, 'This fellow began to build and was not able to finish.' 31 Or what king, going out to wage war against another king, will not sit down first and consider whether he is able with ten thousand to oppose the one who comes against him with twenty thousand? 32 If he cannot, then, while the other is still far away, he sends a delegation and asks for the terms of peace. 33 So therefore, none of you can become my disciple if you do not give up all your possessions.

Who knew that there was a cost associated with being a disciple? I'm not just talking about tithing, I'm not talking about giving up free time. I'm talking about big, life-altering costs. Something important about our Scripture is found in verse 26: *"Whoever comes to me and does not hate father and mother, wife and children, brothers and sisters, yes, and even life itself, cannot be my disciple.*" This does not mean Jesus expects you to have ill feelings towards your relatives or yourself. You see, the word "*hate*" in modern usage has much different context than in Jesus' time. Anytime you see the word "*hate*" in the Bible, it refers to having a preference for one thing over another. In Genesis 29:31 it is said that Jacob "*hated*" his wife Leah, and yet, the context makes it very clear that he merely loved his other wife Rachel "more than" Leah. What Jesus is actually saying here is that you cannot be a disciple if you favor your parents, spouse, children, and yourself over Him. So there's a seminary-level homework assignment for those of you who enjoy bible study at home. Go through the Holy Bible and find as many things as you can that God hates and try to determine what He is actually giving preference to.

Getting back to our Scripture, Jesus explains to us that there is a cost to discipleship that we must be willing to pay.

Like Coach Jim telling us, "I only need those of you who are here to play baseball," Jesus is telling the crowd, "I only need those of you who are here to be disciples." Everything else is second. Cars, homes, tropical vacations, fancy titles reflecting the time and money you've put into your education and profession—the only thing Jesus Christ is going to examine is whether or not you are His disciple.

Coach Jim knew there was a difference between winners and champions. Many people win from time to time. It's a short-lived victory. But champions are committed to learning the game, to following the coach's directions, and to hone their ability to achieve victory time after time. Are you all in? Do you want to be a champion for Christ?

Ephesians 6:1-4:

6:1 Children, obey your parents in the Lord, for this is right. 2"Honor your father and mother," which is the first commandment with promise: 3 "that it may be well with you and you may live long on the earth." 4 And you, fathers, do not provoke your children to wrath, but bring them up in the training and admonition of the Lord. (NKJV)

Fatherhood is certainly something special. Probably the best memories of my life are those I have with my children—hunting trips, mountain climbing, watching them compete in sports, and excel in activities. Even the simple stuff like when we used to play video games together or just talk about things in our lives. But I have found that being a father is not easy. There's been times where I didn't feel like I was a good dad. There's been times where I'm at odds with my kids. There have been times where I worry if my kids are disappointed in me. My father and grandfather shared the same concerns. And I suspect that probably all of us have either been a father who has shared those feelings, or we have had a father whom we felt fell short of our expectations in some way, or was too hard on us. After all, it is no secret that kids don't always see eye-to-eye with their parents.

Regardless of which category you might find yourself in, I have good news: biblically you are not alone. The Bible talks about a lot of stuff, but if there's any one category of people in the Bible, it's fathers. The Bible is full of dads. So let's take a moment to talk about some of these notable dads in Scripture.

We begin, of course, with Adam. Now, admittedly I live a fairly stressful life as I work multiple careers. But let's hand it to Adam, this poor guy had to create the human population. Scripture tells us that Adam and Eve had many children. Now these two had disobeyed God. Imagine going to Adam and Eve's house for a BBQ.

"Hey Adam, I like your place here."

"Yeah, it's alright. But it's not as nice as our last place. We sort messed things up and got kicked out of there. Want a hamburger?"

Despite their disobedience, God still uses Adam and Eve, and they display a great understanding of God's promise. Two of their sons, Cain and Abel, became synonymous with sibling rivalry. Genesis chapter 4 tells us that they had both learned God's promises, which Abel chose to acknowledge while Cain rejected. Free will based on what dad had taught them.

Noah was dad, too. While he was better known as the man tasked with building the ark and saving those who trusted God from the great flood, Noah was also a father. Noah was not always a good father, but his sons and daughters-n-law were by his side during the many years of construction on the ark. And this family stood out to God. At any point during this construction, they could have walked away, but Noah, if nothing else, taught them to trust God. After the flood Noah became a drunkard. I admit, after building a giant ship and spending so much time on the water, I'd probably want to whip up a Margarita or ten myself. But God never relieves or excuses Noah from his responsibilities. Noah goes and gets completely tanked, strips naked, and passes out. What's interesting is that when his three sons find him passed out naked, they don't leave him. Instead, they cover him up, they take care of him.

So, you think things were rough with your dad? Let me tell you about this guy, Abraham. So Abraham and his son, Isaac, are out and about. What Isaac doesn't know is that God had told Abraham to sacrifice Isaac to prove his loyalty. And Abraham intends on doing just that. Now this had not been a particularly contentious relationship between father and son. In fact, Abraham loved Isaac more than anything, which is why God presented this particular challenge. So Abe ties up Isaac, places him on an altar, has the knife in his hand about to kill Isaac...and suddenly God stops Abraham by sending a messenger to intervene having proved his commitment to God. Abe sacrifices a sheep instead. I bet it was quite for a while around the house after that.

Abraham: "Hey, son..."

Isaac: "Shut up, dad. I'm still not talking to you."

Abraham: "Love you..."

Isaac grew up to be a dad himself, instilling the ways God with his own children, that which he had learned from his very, very devout parents.

Then we have King Solomon. Solomon was the wisest guy around, but a terrible father. After all, his father had not been the best role model. In fact, Solomon was such a horrible father that his sons not only turned away from him, they turned away from God. Despite all this, Solomon penned the Book of Proverbs which has been a great teaching tool of wisdom for parents and children for thousands of years.

Moving forward to the New Testament we have Zachariah. Now Zachariah was very old and he and his wife, Elizabeth, had been trying children for a long time, unsuccessfully. Since they had been devoted to God, an angel had been sent to Zachariah informing him that they would be blessed with the birth of a son, John the Baptist. Then Zachariah was made mute and deaf. Nonetheless, his influence on John about the coming Messiah was substantial.

Finally, let's talk about Joseph. What a tribute to step-fathers! His fiancée ends up pregnant, and he is not the father. This guy listens to what God is telling him about the Immaculate Conception, and Jesus being the Messiah, and he toughs it out for the family. Joseph protects Mary and baby Jesus, he even becomes a refugee with them when Herod tries to kill Jesus. Joseph could've cut and run at any time, but he didn't.

You know what these fathers have in common? None of them were perfect. And these are some of the most famous men in world history. There are no perfect dads. The lesson here is that while we may have our shortcomings as fathers, God has given us a purpose. That purpose carries on to our children, and our children's children. Fathers have things that their kids can learn from, things they can teach them. But understand that some of those lessons can only come from an imperfect, flawed dad.

One Sunday morning I addressed my congregations from the pulpit with a large chunk of concrete in my hand: "There are many things we cannot agree about in the Bible. Many, many things. Well I have good news for you, as we are going to talk about something that we can all agree with. In fact, I am so confident that we are in agreement, I will put myself potentially in harm's way. Any of you who believe you have never offended the Lord, any of you who believe you have forever and always lived a completely righteous life, I invite you to come down to the pulpit and pelt me with this stone. I assure you I will not flinch or step out of the way. Are there any takers? Are any of you, who are among us today, completely and perfectly without sin? Again, I ask, are there any takers?"

Thankfully, no one accepted my challenge. I could not cast the stone either. Why is it that none of us could cast the stone? Because we are all aware of the sin in our lives. Since the Garden of Eden, sin has been a part of us, passed on from generation to generation. So if we've done bad things, if we've sinned against our Creator, why is it that we find ourselves here today, all in agreement of our sinfulness? I'll tell you why: because we have received God's mercy.

1 Timothy 1:12-17:

1:12 I am grateful to Christ Jesus our Lord, who has strengthened me, because he judged me faithful and appointed me to his service, 13 even though I was formerly a blasphemer, a persecutor, and a man of violence. But I received mercy because I had acted ignorantly in unbelief, 14 and the grace of our Lord overflowed for me with the faith and love that are in Christ Jesus. 15 The saying is sure and worthy of full acceptance, that Christ Jesus came into the world to save sinners—of whom I am the foremost. 16 But for that very reason I received mercy, so that in me, as the foremost, Jesus Christ might display the utmost patience, making me an example to those who would come to believe in him for eternal life. 17 To the King of the ages, immortal, invisible, the only God, be honor and glory forever and ever. Amen.

1 Timothy is the first of what's known as the three "Pastoral Epistles," which also include 2 Timothy and Titus, all of which are commonly attributed to Paul. The Pastoral Epistles are all about strengthening congregations. But before Paul entered a life a ministry and written these letters, he had lived quite a different type of life, when he was still known as Saul. In our text, Paul confesses that he had not lived a good life. He admits to being a blasphemer, he had been a Pharisee that had denied Jesus as the Christ. He admits to being a persecutor. His job had been to hunt down Christians for the purpose of persecuting them. He further admits that he was a man of violence. He not only persecuted Christians, he imprisoned them, tortured them, even taking part in killing them. Paul uses the story of his past life to point out that even though he had done these terrible things, even though he had been a most wretched sinner, God not only showed him mercy, God called him into His service.

Can you relate to Paul? I certainly can. Mercy. It's one of God's greatest gifts to us. But what is it? Why is it so important? How can we get more of it? In Hebrew, 'mercy' means *'forgiveness.'* It's easy to confuse mercy with grace, but grace is not mercy. It's through God's grace that we receive God's mercy. Understand that mercy is not something we deserve, we're not entitled to it. It's not a get-out-of-jail-free card. God owes us nothing. It is through grace that God shows us mercy.

When I was preparing this lesson, I posed to myself the question, "Why does God show us mercy if we don't deserve it?" As I began to research Scripture in search of the answer, I learned that there were many, many variations of one underlying belief: the idea that if we are forgiven, if we're given another chance, we each have the ability to serve God, to do good things that make the world a slightly better place...just like Paul.

We just observed another anniversary of the September 11th terrorist attacks. The tragedy of that day was not only a shot at America, it was a brutal assault on humanity all across the globe. But beyond the unimaginable horror witnessed on 9/11, we also witnessed humanity in its finest hour. First responders and military personnel, volunteers and everyday citizens sacrificed their lives to rescue people they had never met. The world held its breath as they watched the images on every single television station. People in other parts of the world, who don't speak our language, even people of other faith traditions prayed for America, they prayed for you. People you never met. Aid poured in from around the world. And for the first, and only time in my lifetime, I witnessed our nation united. Mercy flowed like a raging river.

Contrary to the misbeliefs of many, the United States military has been committed to the idea of spreading compassion for many years. One of our largest hospital ships in the world is the USNS Mercy. This 894' long ship has no armament, no weapons, and has 1,000 hospital beds.

Unlike other military vessels, the Mercy is white in color and bears the international symbol of peace and mercy, a red cross. It was first put into service in 1985. Since that time the Mercy has treated over 372,000 patients from over half of the nations in the world, to include prisoners of war. Additionally the Mercy has provided humanitarian aid to numerous foreign countries ravaged by hurricanes, war, and other disasters, and continues to serve to this day. While doing good in the world, in over three decades no enemy force has ever fired upon the USNS Mercy.

Mercy is not deserved, but given freely. Congregations are meant to operate like the USNS Mercy: without expectation of anything in return, with compassion for others regardless of who they are, and with courage knowing that evil may target us at any time. Sharing the mercy that God has given us is not an act of weakness, it's not a political platform, and it's not something we do for show. It's what we are called to do as a congregation of God's servants. Show all the mercy you can, as often as you can, to as many people as you can, as much as you ever can.

Y ou know, after a long day at work I like to come home and relax. For me, listening to music and reading help me leave the day behind. There's a number of things we do and things we have that bring comfort to us. Think about all the things that are out there, things that we have that are meant to make our lives easier or more enjoyable. A few years ago, when my daughter was still a kid living under my roof, I remember she had broken one of my primary rules: school work comes before extracurricular activities. She had spent all of her time at the dance studio and with her friends, and failed to complete several homework assignments. I got an automated message from the school that she had received a couple zeros for not doing the work. In my house, that'll get you busted down.

I decided to ground her, and I remember walking into her room with a grin on my face and asking her, "Hey, what is your most precious possession?"

She looked curiously at me, thought for a minute, and said, "My phone. Why do you ask?"

I said, "It's mine for the rest of the week, hand it over." You'd have thought I was having her executed.

Think about how much we've come to rely on our phones. I can tell you that my phone keeps me connected to work, family, and friends. My calendar is stored on my phone. My pictures and videos. I get my emails, check the weather, watch TV, and access what I believe to be the single most dangerous cancer to society: social media. All the information, entertainment, and technological capabilities we could ever imagine all in this single device that fits in our pocket. And people are willing to spend, on average, $800-$1,000 for a phone. What else do we work our butts off to have?

Cars: have you checked the price of a new car lately?

Houses: according to a major real estate publication, the median price of a home in the Dallas area is currently $379,000.

Food: I remember when I could go on a date to the mall, go see a movie, and eat dinner for forty bucks.

All joking aside, now we spend that on the movie tickets alone. All this inflation keeps going up, the things we want to have and the lifestyles we want to continue keep getting more expensive, so we pursue higher paying jobs, open new credit accounts with lower interest rates, even sometimes we dip into our retirements. But no matter how much money we make, no matter how good of a warranty you buy for that new iPhone, know that there is nothing you can hold in your hand that can't be taken away or destroyed. We come into this world with no possessions of our own, and we leave the same way.

1 Timothy 6:6-19:

6:6 Of course, there is great gain in godliness combined with contentment; 7 for we brought nothing into the world, so that we can take nothing out of it; 8 but if we have food and clothing, we will be content with these. 9 But those who want to be rich fall into temptation and are trapped by many senseless and harmful desires that plunge people into ruin and destruction. 10 For the love of money is a root of all kinds of evil, and in their eagerness to be rich

some have wandered away from the faith and pierced themselves with many pains.

11 But as for you, man of God, shun all this; pursue righteousness, godliness, faith, love, endurance, gentleness. 12 Fight the good fight of the faith; take hold of the eternal life, to which you were called and for which you made the good confession in the presence of many witnesses. 13 In the presence of God, who gives life to all things, and of Christ Jesus, who in his testimony before Pontius Pilate made the good confession, I charge you 14 to keep the commandment without spot or blame until the manifestation of our Lord Jesus Christ, 15 which he will bring about at the right time—he who is the blessed and only Sovereign, the King of kings and Lord of lords. 16 It is he alone who has immortality and dwells in unapproachable light, whom no one has ever seen or can see; to him be honor and eternal dominion. Amen.

17 As for those who in the present age are rich, command them not to be haughty, or to set their hopes on the uncertainty of riches, but rather on God who richly provides us with everything for our enjoyment. 18 They are to do good, to be rich in good works, generous, and ready to share, 19 thus storing up for themselves the treasure of a good foundation for the future, so that they may take hold of the life that really is life.

On September 11, 2019, the billionaire oil-tycoon and philanthropist T. Boone Pickens passed away. I've spent a lot of time examining the works of others, taking note of their successes and failures, and I'll tell you I think this man had it figured out. Well-known for his generous giving, Pickens was also a philosopher of sorts. He left behind a final message for the world to hear, and in that message he stresses one key realization: it's not what you have, it's how people will remember you after you've passed on. He goes on to quote one of his favorite poems called *"Indispensable Man"* written by Saxon White Kessinger in 1959.

T. Boone Pickens, who was a man of faith, knew that he would return to the earth just as he had come into it: with nothing.

Big houses, nice cars, retirement accounts, great friends and family, healthy-fit bodies, and yes, even that $800 iPhone…none of it will matter on that day when you gasp your final breath of air and close your eyes for the last time in your mortal life. Standing before God in our time of judgement, without any of our possessions, without our money, without our friends and family, without that damned iPhone that we couldn't live without, the only thing that will matter is how we served God and observed His ordinances.

Life is fairly short and being content is fine. But we must be aware of where our investments are going. Are our priorities on making ourselves comfortable, or serving God? Are we leaving behind possessions, or legacies for the betterment of the world? Are we spending our lives chasing temporary treasures, or a life everlasting?

"Together Around the World"

On the first Sunday in October we celebrate World Communion Sunday. Christian churches all over the world are joined together on this day to take part in the sacrament of Communion. For us it may not seem all that out of the ordinary since we generally take Communion on the first Sunday of each month. But the truth of the matter is that many other denominations do not take Communion the same way, many of which only have Communion on special holidays. So rejoice as we share Communion with other denominations in Russia, Great Britain, Honduras, Ghana, China, Fiji—places all over the globe. Blessing the elements...together. Reciting the liturgy...together. And most importantly, seeking God's grace and forgiveness...together...because as children of God we lament together.

We may not find ourselves all lamenting about the same problems. The Ebola virus is not an epidemic in the USA, but it is somewhere. The vast majority of Texans are not living in makeshift huts, but that's the case somewhere. War has not left our community in crumbles, but somewhere it has. But for as many different suffrages that we can name, there are those that we share as well, like losing a loved one, or when marriages become difficult, or when we are afraid, or guilt-stricken, or lost. We share the lamentations of our brothers and sisters in Christ who have joined together to pray for God to change something, joined together to share hope in the Lord. We are one denomination, from one single race of people, all of one single nationality, all speaking the same language...the language of prayer.

Lamentations 3:19-26:

3:19 The thought of my affliction and my homelessness

is wormwood and gall!

20 My soul continually thinks of it

and is bowed down within me.

21 But this I call to mind,

and therefore I have hope:

22 The steadfast love of the Lord never ceases,

his mercies never come to an end;

23 they are new every morning;

great is your faithfulness.

24 "The Lord is my portion," says my soul,

"therefore I will hope in him."

25 The Lord is good to those who wait for him,

to the soul that seeks him.

26 It is good that one should wait quietly

for the salvation of the Lord.

The book of Lamentations is a small book in the Old Testament following Jeramiah. We believe that it was written by Jeramiah, but we're not certain. What we are certain of is that the book consists of five lamenting poems, written by someone who witnessed the destruction of Jerusalem by the Babylonians around the year 586 BC. Imagine your community being sieged by a foreign invader, your family and friends being killed, all the buildings being burned down, everything you've known is gone. That's what the author is lamenting about in this book.

But the book of Lamentations is not about being sad or discouraged with the situation, it's about finding hope through faith in God. In 2012, Jan was an attractive, successful Assistant District Attorney for a large metropolitan area. Her career was going well, she was in great health, and was enjoying life with her boyfriend, Gary. Jan had it all going for her. One evening she comes home, unlocks the door to her apartment, and her dog rushes out to greet her. Jan was caught off-guard, lost her balance, staggered backwards, and fell through the railing behind her. She fell nearly twenty feet, crashing down to the ground below. When she opened her eyes, she said she couldn't move. Jan was placed in a medically induced coma, and when was awoke in her hospital bed, her Gary told her that the doctors had done all they could for her, but she would never walk again and would always be paralyzed from the chest down. She said at that point all she could do was have faith in God. Less than three months later, she walked out of the rehabilitation center she'd been in. She got married, and had a baby which she was able to deliver naturally. Jan says she was given a second chance because even when she was paralyzed, she never stopped walking with God.

It's rare that a day goes by that I don't get a text message or phone call from someone in need of prayer. Naturally, these requests are sent to me because I'm a pastor. In addition to prayer, I almost always refer the request to other members of the congregation or community. Why do I do that? Think about it like a congregational prayer circle, where together we all lay our hands on those in need of prayer. It's a connection. That's what we do on World Communion Sunday.

October is a busy month. We celebrate the fall season. We celebrate Halloween. We observe Breast Cancer Awareness. It's also the month we observe Domestic Violence Awareness. While there's a lot of coverage on spousal abuse during this period, we shouldn't forget about the other form of domestic violence: child abuse. Which is what I want to talk about now because it's been such a part of our ministry and there's still a lot of work to be done to prevent it. Unlike drug abuse or spousal abuse, child abuse is something that we directly intervene in and put a stop to. Child abuse is the most vile, inexcusable form evil that one person can afflict on another, and we need to know what the Bible says about it.

First, you need to know that studies show that one in four children in America are victims of abuse. Mathematically that means that many of the people you know were likely victims of abuse as a child. Approximately four children die from abuse every day in the US. That might not sound like all that many, but that comes out to over 1,400 children each year. To put that into perspective, that's more deaths than those sustained by the US military in combat, law enforcement line of duty deaths, and firefighter line of duty deaths...combined. And of those child deaths, 70% of the children were under the age of three. And if you think child abuse ends when children grow up, you wrong. It has permanent lasting effects that are often passed on to the next generation. Additionally, 14% of men and 36% of women in prison were victims of child abuse. It's like a footprint in wet cement. Child abuse comes in many forms: physical abuse, sexual abuse, emotional abuse, verbal abuse, and educational neglect are the most common. So what can the church do to stop child abuse? Why should we get involved?

2 Timothy 2:8-15:

2:8 Remember Jesus Christ, raised from the dead, a descendant of David—that is my gospel, 9 for which I suffer hardship, even to the point of being chained like a criminal. But the word of God is not chained. 10 Therefore I endure everything for the sake of the elect, so that they may also obtain the salvation that is in Christ Jesus, with eternal glory. 11 The saying is sure:

If we have died with him, we will also live with him;

12 if we endure, we will also reign with him;

if we deny him, he will also deny us;

13 if we are faithless, he remains faithful—

for he cannot deny himself.

14 Remind them of this, and warn them before God that they are to avoid wrangling over words, which does no good but only ruins those who are listening. 15 Do your best to present yourself to God as one approved by him, a worker who has no need to be ashamed, rightly explaining the word of truth.

The Bible often makes references of children being the embodiment of the true nature of God. Thus, Jesus explained that the way we treat children is how we treat God. Jesus was a staunch defender of children, and warned of severe consequences for anyone who harmed children.

Mark 9:42 says, *"If any of you put a stumbling block before one of these little ones who believe in me, it would*

169

be better for you if a great millstone were hung around your neck and you were thrown into the sea."

Why was Jesus so passionate about it? Think about it. Jesus was the descendant of sexually exploited women, he was a survivor of a genocide that specifically targeted children, and then there's the fact that children, in his time, were considered property rather than people.

Thankfully our attitude has changed towards children. But defeating the evil that is child abuse requires us to take action. Our text instructs us to be a worker approved by God. The church must continue to be a sanctuary. We can do that by standing against all forms of child abuse, reporting suspected abuse to authorities, and supporting the organizations that protect children: organizations like Court Appointed Special Advocates (CASA) and the regional Child Advocacy Centers. Educating new parents on appropriate child care methods helps reduce neglect. Finally, make the church a 'safe place' for children, a place where they know they are welcome, and a place where they can find help. We will, at last, see them as representatives of God, and as we welcome these children, we will also be welcoming Christ.

"Cassette Tapes"

Childhood is an amazing time. I didn't have to pay for anything. Everything was new and exciting. My imagination worked a lot better back then. Hopefully we all have some fond memories of childhood. I remember taking these long road trips with mom up to see my grandparents in Pennsylvania. Mom was a teacher, so we'd have summers off together and we would take the scenic route. The earliest road trip up there I can remember was when I was about five or six years old. We had this ugly Nissan van. Man, that thing was hideous, but it sure was comfortable. Inside that van was something that intrigued me: it was called a cassette player. Now, there's only so much highway you can stare at on a 1,200 mile trip before you get mind-numbingly bored, but mom would put in a cassette and we'd listen to music. I remember cruising through the Smokey Mountains to the sounds of Paul Simon, David Holt, and Harry Belefonte. Even today, any time I go up that way or see a picture of those mountains I think of those songs. Since that time, I've noticed that I associate a strong connection between music and family. Those old cassettes became part of my DNA, an imprint of who and what I grew up to be. Can you think of anything from your childhood that has such an effect on you still to this day?

Let me throw in the clutch and shift gears for a moment. I think it's safe to say that, as a people, we live in a world divided. All these different religions, politics, races and classes of people, even our favorite sports teams. But instead of standing here and just pointing out how divided we are, I want to focus on what unites us. In Luke 18:9-14 Jesus tells the parable of the Pharisee and the Tax-Collector.

18:9 He also told this parable to some who trusted in themselves that they were righteous and regarded others with contempt: 10 "Two men went up to the temple to pray, one a Pharisee and the other a tax collector. 11 The Pharisee, standing by himself, was praying thus, 'God, I thank you that I am not like other people: thieves, rogues, adulterers, or even like this tax collector. 12 I fast twice a week; I give a tenth of all my income.' 13 But the tax collector, standing far off, would not even look up to heaven, but was beating his breast and saying, 'God, be merciful to me, a sinner!' 14 I tell you, this man went down to his home justified rather than the other; for all who exalt themselves will be humbled, but all who humble themselves will be exalted."

Here you have two people from two very different backgrounds. First, you have the Pharisee. He has a position of power. He has more money than most people. He eats the best food. He has a very strict faith-system. This is a man who follows the law of Scripture to the tee. And in doing so he lives a segregated life apart from those who are not like him. Like the second man in this parable. This man is a tax collector. Tax collectors were considered to be the lowest of the low. While they were not only often crooked, over-taxing people and stealing their money, they worked for the Romans, the very people who ran the oppressive regime. If you didn't pay the tax collector what he said you have to pay, he would report you to the Romans, who would then imprison or possibly even execute you for disobeying a servant of the Empire. The tax collector was seen as a traitor, a thief, scum of the earth. The Pharisee is praying to God, thanking Him for not making him like the tax collector. He thinks God favors him over this tax collector, and thinks pretty highly of himself. Now, the tax collector knows he has sinned, he knows that he is not worthy of God's grace.

He's on his knees crying out to the Lord, "God, have mercy on me even though I've sinned!" Jesus explains that it is in fact the tax collector who is justified in this parable. But He doesn't just disregard the Pharisee. It doesn't say God condemned him to Hell, it doesn't say he destroyed him. No, the Pharisee is humbled by the Lord and placed on the same level as the lowly tax collector.

In the Medieval period, the church wasn't anything like it is today. Nations competed to gain the favor of the church. They used money, they gave large pieces of real estate to the bishops. Wars were fought for control over the church. Likewise, the church was notorious for creating its own wars, which often resulted in famine, torture, and corruption. Thousands upon thousands died. If you were poor you couldn't go to church. If you were an unwedded woman a child you couldn't go to church. If you supported the wrong political party you couldn't go to church. This is what prompted the Reformation. The Reformation brought God back to the center of the church. Corruption was stomped out, common folks like us were allowed to come worship together, and it was made accessible to everyone. And that's the word of the day: *Everyone.*

In many ways, all of us are either the Pharisee or the tax collector. We will either be humbled, or we humble ourselves. On that Day of Judgment, Pharisee and tax collector are both God's children. While we are a society of divided people, we all need God's grace. None of us deserve it more than any other. And God loves His children—all of them. Even the ones we don't like and the ones who don't like us. When everything else about us is different, this is what unites us. Like that DNA imprint from my childhood with music being something that helps unify my family, God's ever-present love for us, and our need for Him.

Luke 19:1-10:

19:1 He entered Jericho and was passing through it. 2 A man was there named Zacchaeus; he was a chief tax collector and was rich. 3 He was trying to see who Jesus was, but on account of the crowd he could not, because he was short in stature. 4 So he ran ahead and climbed a sycamore tree to see him, because he was going to pass that way. 5 When Jesus came to the place, he looked up and said to him, "Zacchaeus, hurry and come down; for I must stay at your house today." 6 So he hurried down and was happy to welcome him. 7 All who saw it began to grumble and said, "He has gone to be the guest of one who is a sinner." 8 Zacchaeus stood there and said to the Lord, "Look, half of my possessions, Lord, I will give to the poor; and if I have defrauded anyone of anything, I will pay back four times as much." 9 Then Jesus said to him, "Today salvation has come to this house, because he too is a son of Abraham. 10 For the Son of Man came to seek out and to save the lost."

A while back I was at a concert down in Dallas supporting one of my lifelong friends who is a musician. There were several other friends in my group who'd known each other for about thirty-five years. One of the guys had left our group to go to the bathroom, and when he returned he told us that he had seen one of our old friends named Jay down by the stage. Now, the last time I'd seen Jay I think we were around fourteen years old. Jay was an overweight kid, he was pretty popular, and he was a class clown. During our sophomore year in high school, Jay got in trouble with

175

drugs and ended up dropping out of school. That was the last I'd seen him. I decided to go down and say hi. When I got down where I was told he was, I looked around but I didn't see him anywhere.

Finally my buddy came over and pointed to a man sitting about eight feet away and said, "That's him."

I thought to myself, "No way!" He didn't look anything like I remembered. He was thin, appeared to be fit, and had aged about twenty-five years. He just looked at me when I reached out to shake his hand. I could tell he was trying to figure out who I was. Then it dawned on me, the last time he saw me I was stick-thin, about a hundred pounds lighter, with braces and long hair. I, too had aged about twenty-five years. Talking to him I found out he'd gone to a trade school and had a successful career, wife, and kids. It was as if he were someone else. Do you believe that you are the same person that you have always been?

All Saints/All Souls Sunday is the Sunday following All Saints Day on November 1st. This particular Sunday we remember the Saints who paved the way to Christ for us, as well as all the other regular people who helped shape our faith and have passed on. John Wesley, although not Catholic, always stressed recognition and a show of appreciation for the Saints for the impact they've had on Christianity, and such has been a Methodist tradition since the formation of the church. Some time back I had been thinking about which Saints had been most influential on me. I thought about Saint Paul. I thought about Saint Patrick. I thought about Saint John of the Cross and a few others. Then I thought about the regular people. I thought about my grandfather. I thought about my friend, Greg. I thought about my step-mother, Ronda. All had passed on, but had played a part in my faith.

It was in that moment that another person came to mind. Someone who had probably more to do with my faith today than any other person. I could vividly see this person in my memory. This man was not a particularly good person, in the past he had lied to me a lot, he beat me up a few times, he had at times scared me. He did not submit himself to Christ. But it was this man who convinced me that *I* should.

It was because of this man that I walked into a church building just a little ways south of here, for the first time in many years and I told the pastor there, "I want to come back. I want to know Jesus again." That man was me. The manifestation of a former life that had passed away. I can recall times where I would do whatever I could to conceal that man and the things he'd done. I didn't want the world to know him. He was dead and that was it. But that turned out to be incorrect, that wasn't it. You see, that man, like the Saints, like our dearly departed, had played an instrumental role in my personal faith walk. The ghosts of our past also live in our present, and whether we realize it or not, we do live with them. As we share communion, let us also reflect on our former lives that have passed away, just like the tax collector, Zaccaeus, who'd both been looked down upon physically and morally as nothing more than a sinner, but yet kept the company of Christ in his home and in his heart.

"The Man Who Did Nothing"

A young man who thought he was so smart that he could sit upon his father's porch day after day and do nothing. For he was to inherit his family's great wealth. He need not do a single thing. So the young man, believing he was preserving his marvelous life sat upon that porch and did nothing. One day a beautiful young lady walked past the porch on her way to town. Day after day she walked by, catching the man's eye, but yet, he did nothing. The beautiful young lady went on to marry another man because the man on the porch merely watched as she passed by...and did nothing. A young school boy who was meant to grow up to bring great joy to others, eventually beginning a family of his own, would never exist, because the man on the porch had missed his chance to marry what would have been the boy's mother. He merely sat on the porch...and did nothing.

Then, one day an Army recruiter came to the man on the porch and said, "Sir, are you interested in a career in the Army?"

Waving him off, the man on the porch just sat there...and did nothing. Several years later, a mother in another part of the country was being informed that her only son had died from a wound he sustained in battle. You see, the medic that was to save her son's life by applying life-saving medicine had never joined the Army. He just sat on the porch...and did nothing.

Later, a man in a suit walks up to the man on the porch and says, "Hey friend, can you help me find a ride across town to my office? My car broke down just up the street and I have a very important meeting that I'm going to miss if I can't get a ride."

The man on the porch just shook his head...and did nothing. The man in the suit dashed off toward his office, but by the time he had gotten there he had missed the important meeting. Meanwhile, seven men and three women walked into their houses earlier than usual, just to tell their families that they had lost their jobs. Their boss had failed to show up at a meeting with corporate to lobby for them to be able to keep their jobs while the company was downsizing...all because the man on the porch...did nothing. Finally, when the man on the porch had become old and feeble, he looked around and became saddened. He had believed himself to be so smart: he had inherited great wealth and all he had to do was be alive and do nothing. And in the end he realized that he had no heir because he had no family, he had never had a career, he never had any friends, he never made an impact on anyone's life, ever. All because he did nothing. He gets dizzy, can't seem to catch his breath, and begins to fall onto the deck of that porch. All goes dark. Then his eyes open, and sitting before him is a ghostly, powerful figure, surrounded by bright light.

"This is it! Truly I am before the King of Kings! Master, let me walk with you in the Kingdom of Heaven!" he thought to himself.

But his eyes begin to adjust, and the ghostly figure comes into focus. Why, it wasn't a king at all. It was just a plain man. A man that looked just like he did, sitting on a porch. And the man...did nothing.

2 Thessalonians 3:6-13:

3:6 Now we command you, beloved, in the name of our Lord Jesus Christ, to keep away from believers who are living in idleness and not according to the tradition that they received from us. 7 For you yourselves know how you ought to imitate us; we were not idle when we were with you, 8 and we did not eat anyone's bread without paying for it; but with toil and labor we worked night and day, so that we might not burden any of you. 9 This was not because we do not have that right, but in order to give you an example to imitate. 10 For even when we were with you, we gave you this command: Anyone unwilling to work should not eat. 11 For we hear that some of you are living in idleness, mere busybodies, not doing any work. 12 Now such persons we command and exhort in the Lord Jesus Christ to do their work quietly and to earn their own living. 13 Brothers and sisters, do not be weary in doing what is right.

I was led to share this story with you as an example of how God has many purposes for us in our lives. When we find something that we're good at or that we're passionate about, we tend to focus on that one particular thing. Hence the term, "my purpose in life." But the truth that God wants you to know is that He has many, many purposes for you. Some are big and obvious, while some are small and unnoticeable. But any and all of these purposes can have a significant impact. What purpose does God have for your life right now?

There's a lot of people in the secular world that seem to think that society owes them something for nothing. Likewise, there are many Christians who believe that God owes them something for nothing. Neither of which are correct. There is a difference though, while we might have to work a bit harder for what we receive in the secular world, grace is offered to us freely. That doesn't mean we don't have to do something for it. We have to submit ourselves to Christ, and we have to be willing to receive God's grace.

In my hometown of Farmersville, Texas we have an annual community event called 'Old Time Saturday.' It's the first Saturday of every October. It's become quite a big event, and everyone seems to come to it. I remember, as a kid, going to Old Time Saturday and getting excited about the "Quarter in a Haystack" game. Now, this game is pretty simple. There's a big pile of hay with a bunch of quarters in it. The referee (or whatever he's called) would blow a whistle and all the kids would jump into the haystack and dig around for the quarters. And if you were really lucky, you found a silver dollar. At the end of the game, whatever you found, you got to keep. Man, it was exciting!

Grace is like the quarters in the haystack. It's exciting. It's free for the taking. But we have to go out and get it. Idleness prevents us from finding and receiving grace. The reason Paul sent the message to the Thessalonians that we read in our text was that many of them had a misunderstanding about grace and the return of Christ. They had believed that because they had been forgiven of their sins, they had no further need to work or earn wages. But Paul reminds them that working is a divine task that God has assigned to all human beings. Living a life of idleness, of handouts and freebies, is not a divine lifestyle. God does not intend for us to live off of the government, or our spouse, or our parents, or anyone. And the consequences may affect other people that you don't even realize were part of the bigger picture. If you're disabled or living off a pension, that's one thing—it's not always about money. There are still many other things we can do. We have many purposes in our lives. We don't always know what they are, or where we might find them, but we can't just sit on the porch. If we're going to find any quarters in the haystack, we've got to get off of the porch.

"Semper Fidelis"

D o you know what happened on November 10th in the year 1775? That's the year that the United States Marine Corps was born in Tun Tavern in Philadelphia. Semper Fidelis: the Marine Corps motto. It means *"always faithful."* Joining the Marine Corps was something I had mixed feelings about. Part of me was afraid. I think I was afraid that I would fail. Maybe a little bit afraid of being horribly maimed or killed, but not so much. Maybe I was afraid just because it was something so much bigger than me. But the other part of me was proud and excited. I was going to be a Marine. I was going to wear the dress blues. I was going to be part of the Marine Corps legacy.

I signed up when I was seventeen years old and people asked me, "Why did you pick the Marines? Why not the Army or the Navy?" I'll tell you why. To me the Marine Corps was the best. I looked up to them. When the nation needed a hero, someone to call on, they called in the Marines. I wanted to be a part of that. My excitement about being a U.S. Marine outweighed the fears I had about it.

One of our most human characteristics is the fact that from an early age we become aware of our mortality. Around the same time we also learn what is right from wrong. Within us, a spiritual battlefield is created that will exist for the duration of our whole lives. While we know we are to trust God, evil will continue to make every attempt to steer us off course with lies and regret. And if we're not careful we find ourselves worrying about our destination. We ask questions like, "Will it hurt when I die? Will God judge me harshly? What if it none of it happens the way I've

183

imagined? What if Jesus doesn't come back for me and I'm left behind?"

2 Thessalonians 2:1-5, 13-17:

2:1 As to the coming of our Lord Jesus Christ and our being gathered together to him, we beg you, brothers and sisters, 2 not to be quickly shaken in mind or alarmed, either by spirit or by word or by letter, as though from us, to the effect that the day of the Lord is already here. 3 Let no one deceive you in any way; for that day will not come unless the rebellion comes first and the lawless one is revealed, the one destined for destruction. 4 He opposes and exalts himself above every so-called god or object of worship, so that he takes his seat in the temple of God, declaring himself to be God. 5 Do you not remember that I told you these things when I was still with you?

13 But we must always give thanks to God for you, brothers and sisters beloved by the Lord, because God chose you as the first fruits for salvation through sanctification by the Spirit and through belief in the truth. 14 For this purpose he called you through our proclamation of the good news, so that you may obtain the glory of our Lord Jesus Christ. 15 So then, brothers and sisters, stand firm and hold fast to the traditions that you were taught by us, either by word of mouth or by our letter.

16 Now may our Lord Jesus Christ himself and God our Father, who loved us and through grace gave us eternal comfort and good hope, 17 comfort your hearts and strengthen them in every good work and word.

So what is the bottom line of what Paul is saying here? Does your *want* outweigh your fear? There's some bad theology out there. I think one of the most dangerous is

184

the idea that everyone gets to go to Heaven unconditionally. That simply is not true. We have to want it. We have to pursue that eternal life. God doesn't keep us from everlasting life in His Kingdom, *we* do. Grace alone is sufficient for our salvation. To be justified is to be "made right." In the process of salvation, this means we're liberated from the guilt and punishment of our sin and have our souls renewed in the image of God. Only the presence and power of God in our lives can free us from the guilt and punishment of sin. All we have to do is hold fast to our faith. Remain faithful—always faithful. Semper Fidelis. Await the return of Jesus Christ with patience.

"The Good King"

Thanksgiving is that time of year when American tradition poses to us the question, "What are you thankful for?" I was asked that very question. "What are you thankful for this year?" When I was asked that question my mind was on other stuff, I was in the middle of some report writing. Initially I was slightly annoyed by the interruption, but then it dawned on me that I needed to be pondering that question each and every day. Admittedly these past couple years have been more difficult for me than others. I had some hard knocks. I'd lost family. Mostly things that I haven't shared publicly. When I was asked, "What am I thankful for this year," those were my initial thoughts: not what I had been blessed with, but what I had been dealing with. And it was about that time that God smacked me upside the head. I'm blessed in so many ways that I can't even begin to list them all.

I recall a bit of shame about my attitude having watched an interview with a middle-aged woman who had been a victim of human trafficking since she was fifteen years old. She had been forced to used intravenous drugs against her will, she'd had multiple abortions, and she'd been raped over and over and over by men three times her age. She described a time when she was a dollar and a half short of her daily quota and her pimp locked her in a basement where she spent the entire night fighting off starving dogs to keep them from eating her. Part of her leg was torn off by the beasts. What was this tortured woman's final message? She was thankful to God for being alive and being able to escape that life. Even with so much unimaginable pain and suffering, she recognized the blessings that a loving and gracious God had given her. The worst day in Heaven is better than the best day in Hell. That's right, no sugar-coated feel-good preaching here folks. Just raw truths.

So when we think of Thanksgiving what some things we think about? Eating? Turkey? Family? Football? I'll tell you what, I think the Thanksgiving holiday is probably one of the most universally celebrated Christian observances we have. I have some friends of another faith tradition that prepare a big feast for Thanksgiving, using their own traditional foods rather than Turkey.

I asked the husband, "If you aren't Christian, why do you celebrate Thanksgiving?"

He said, "Although we worship God differently, God has blessed us all equally. The American Thanksgiving tradition is one we can celebrate together, thanks to God."

He was absolutely correct. We tend to think of the Pilgrims as some western Europeans who made friends with the Indians and held a big feast in honor of a successful harvest. Such is not the case friends. The Pilgrims were essentially the tortured woman in the interview I'd watched. These people, these Christians, had been mistreated, abused, persecuted, even tortured and killed in some regions. They were from England, Germany, France, Norway, Ireland. They suffered great losses crossing the Atlantic Ocean. The mortality rate for the voyage was one out of three. Infant mortality was even higher at three out of four. They left their homelands, knowing they would likely not see their loved ones again who stayed behind. Those that survived the voyage established communities that struggled to get the crops and livestock to stay alive. Hostile Indians would raid villages, steal children, and murder their parents. Survival was a challenge…a serious one. It was a result of these challenges that brought to life the words of Paul in Colossians 1:11-20 for these Pilgrims, these survivors. Read Paul's thanksgiving and declaration of the supremacy of Christ.

1:11 May you be made strong with all the strength that comes from his glorious power, and may you be prepared to endure everything with patience, while joyfully 12 giving thanks to the Father, who has enabled you to share in the inheritance of the saints in the light. 13 He has rescued us from the power of darkness and transferred us into the kingdom of his beloved Son, 14 in whom we have redemption, the forgiveness of sins.

15 He is the image of the invisible God, the firstborn of all creation; 16 for in him all things in heaven and on earth were created, things visible and invisible, whether thrones or dominions or rulers or powers—all things have been created through him and for him. 17 He himself is before all things, and in him all things hold together. 18 He is the head of the body, the church; he is the beginning, the firstborn from the dead, so that he might come to have first place in everything. 19 For in him all the fullness of God was pleased to dwell, 20 and through him God was pleased to reconcile to himself all things, whether on earth or in heaven, by making peace through the blood of his cross.

Pilgrims and Puritans who had come to New England to start a new way of life had been used to living under the King of England, specifically King Charles I. These were the King's subjects. But they served another king—Christ the King. These two kings ruled differently. Both claim supremacy. Charles commanded loyalty, under penalty of imprisonment or death. Christ commanded loyalty through free will. Charles was notoriously self-righteous. Christ knew all people were flawed and offered grace. Charles kept his people weak in order to control them. Christ made weak people strong. Charles promised English rule for his subjects that ultimately ended in civil war. Christ promised eternal life, and gives eternal life.

There is only one Supreme King who rules with fairness, justice, grace, and mercy. Through Him we are made wise and strong. And to Him we should be thankful, every single day.

My oldest kid, Jacob, seemed to always be getting into trouble. He was a sweet kid, but always causing mischief. Since the time he was three years old, he was like Dennis the Menace. He would go in his room and close the door. We had a rule about not closing the door, so when I would notice the door closed, I would open it. Before I did that though, I would listen to see if I could hear anything. When toddlers are silent, they're usually up to no good. If I heard no sound, I'd swing the door open and he'd have that "deer-in-the-headlights" look on his face. Parents know that look. That single expression says, "Uh oh!"

Now, think back to 6:00 PM last night. I have no idea what you were doing. But imagine that you were doing it, whatever it was, and suddenly Jesus is there. Right at that very moment. Are you squared away? Or did you have that "deer-in-the-headlights" look? You might be thinking, "I wonder what the preacher was doing. Was he praying? Was he reading his Bible?" No, I was actually breaking my diet by eating some spaghetti. I just wanted some spaghetti. So that's that.

We have officially launched a brand new Christian liturgical year. Biblical history teaches us that the Advent season was about preparing for the arrival of Jesus into the world. This was a life-changing event. For us, a practical observation of this season focuses on Christ's return, or His arrival into our lives. Also a life-changing event. And because Christ's impact on our lives is holy, the way we celebrate Jesus should remain holy. The holiday season is an exciting time. Kids and adults alike tend to look forward to it. What's not to like? The family gatherings, the presents, the food... Great times! But for many people the holidays are anything but holy. We see a spike in crime during this season. One of the top crimes is drunk driving. We see a spike in domestic violence calls. We see people who know Christ begin to stumble a bit. With all the chaos and hoopla over the season, many people just want it to end. Why? The family gatherings, the presents, the food...you get the idea. Kids, you will never know how hard your parents struggled to make sure you had a memorable Christmas experience. Parents, it wasn't any easier for your folks when you were a kid. But the result, not the gifts, is what made it all worthwhile. So what does Paul say about how Christians should behave while awaiting Jesus?

Romans 13:11-14.

13:11 Besides this, you know what time it is, how it is now the moment for you to wake from sleep. For salvation is nearer to us now than when we became believers; 12 the night is far gone, the day is near. Let us then lay aside the works of darkness and put on the armor of light; 13 let us live honorably as in the day, not in reveling and drunkenness, not in debauchery and licentiousness, not in quarreling and jealousy. 14 Instead, put on the Lord Jesus Christ, and make no provision for the flesh, to gratify its desires.

Each year we join in the traditional Hanging of the Greens. Now, this particular tradition isn't biblical in origin. It started in the 1500's. But what it symbolizes *is* biblical. The evergreen symbolizing a God of all seasons, the wreaths symbolizing eternal life, the Christmon Tree, the cedar, the holly...all representing biblical principles. But if I had to sum up what all this holiday stuff represents, I'd say ultimately it represents God's love. Thus, our behavior for this season should reflect love. And let me clarify what "love" means. Biblical love means that we put others' well-being first, not our own. One thing that irritates me is preaching that teaches people to love someone because loving others gets us into heaven. Christian love means that we love someone because we want them to go to heaven. That's the kind of love we're talking about here. So, in the spirit of this Advent season, here are some ways that you can celebrate Christ with love.

1) Give money or goods to someone who does not have them. If you can, pick charities that contribute to the relief of others throughout the year.

2) Spend a few moments with those in your household weekly, or daily, and reflect on the things that you're thankful for over the past year. Thanksgiving doesn't end in November.

3) Prepare meals, with, not for, family and friends. One of the oldest traditions in human history is preparing and eating meals together. Christ wants unity for us, celebrate it with food.

4) Visit other churches and faith traditions. African-American, Latin, Catholic...all these congregations celebrate Christ in different ways, but Christ loves us all the same. Each congregation has something to spiritually offer.

5) Buy gifts that are meaningful and appropriate. The first Christmas gift was Jesus. Every Christmas gift you buy is an abstract representation of God's gift of Jesus to us. Think about that before you buy a violent video game or a bottle of booze, or whatever. Nerf guns are the exception, they

promote parental involvement with their kids and they don't hurt much.

Matthew 1:18-25

1:18 Now the birth of Jesus the Messiah took place in this way. When his mother Mary had been engaged to Joseph, but before they lived together, she was found to be with child from the Holy Spirit. 19 Her husband Joseph, being a righteous man and unwilling to expose her to public disgrace, planned to dismiss her quietly. 20 But just when he had resolved to do this, an angel of the Lord appeared to him in a dream and said, "Joseph, son of David, do not be afraid to take Mary as your wife, for the child conceived in her is from the Holy Spirit. 21 She will bear a son, and you are to name him Jesus, for he will save his people from their sins." 22 All this took place to fulfill what had been spoken by the Lord through the prophet:

23 "Look, the virgin shall conceive and bear a son, and they shall name him Emmanuel, which means, "God is with us." 24 When Joseph awoke from sleep, he did as the angel of the Lord commanded him; he took her as his wife, 25 but had no marital relations with her until she had borne a son; and he named him Jesus.

One thing about growing up around this part of the world is that we love our parades. We have parades for every holiday, we have parades for homecoming, we have parades for Veterans—we just have a lot of parades! And that's a good thing, I think. I like parades. It's cool to see everyone get together to celebrate. Such has been a tradition since the days of the Old Testament. But you know, I think hands-down my favorite parade is always the Christmas parade back in my hometown. The town square is decorated,

Christmas lights are shining all around, music is playing, and all the people would come to see the parade. They would stop what they're doing, whatever might be going on in their lives, to come see the Christmas parade. You can look around and see God in the faces of the crowd. I remember when Ronda was going through chemo and had lost all her hair, and she was bundled up really well because it was chilly but she wanted to see the parade. She wasn't the only one. I've seen soldiers on leave from their military campaigns in hostile regions, standing there on the sidewalk with their loved ones, enjoying their short time together before they have to go back. I've seen parents holding their babies, seeing their first parade. I've seen children holding their elderly parents who came to watch their last one. The sights and sounds were like no other time of the year. All the people come to see the parade and for that one, brief moment each year, it seemed that time just stopped. The marching band plays holiday tunes and the firetruck's siren wails, people on decorated floats waving to their friends on the sidewalks, and every face in the crowd had a smile on it. It seemed to be something that made people and families whole again. If only we could just live in that one happy moment for the rest of our lives.

One of the crowd favorites, and also one of mine, are the classic cars. Magnificent machines from different periods in history rumble down the parade route. One year I had an epiphany. An old 1920's Model T Ford drove by, shining, pristine, with a Christmas wreath on the grille. No detail had been ignored. This thing was amazing. Then I thought about where it had been, what it had been through. I could only imagine since it was built how many storms it had survived. It had seen a number of wars. How many dents and dings it had over the years. Nearly 100 years in existence, and yet this thing drives by me just as shiny as it was the day it was first bought. The reality is that it wasn't always shiny and new. It got hit by hail, it had rust spots, it had bumped into things and got dented up, parts had worn out and fallen apart. This Model T had been a restoration project. Through love and commitment, new life had been given to this car, keeping it going. When something else breaks on it, it gets fixed and keeps going.

Did you know that Jesus is doing the same thing in your life? Since Adam and Eve, humanity has exposed itself to some pretty harsh elements, rusting away our souls. That has been the case of nearly every biblical civilization, every figure mentioned in Scripture. Throughout history humans have struggled with sin, with pain and suffering, war, famine, debauchery, hatred. Humanity prayed for a relief, prayed for God to intervene. The prophet Isaiah, along with many others, foretold of a new covenant that would restore us to a graceful state. Christ is that covenant. As we break down, as the years pass us by, as we feel like we start to rust away, Jesus makes us new again. And here's the great part: it doesn't happen just once. Just like any good restoration project, Jesus continually works on us, day after day after day, until one day we are completely restored. Like the Christmas parade, this is the season to look around and enjoy the visible tributes to the birth of Our Savior. But realize that where we hold parades with cars and firetrucks and marching bands, Jesus puts us on parade. We are His masterpieces, He has put His love and commitment into fixing us and keeping us going. Yes, Christ can heal the world. Yes, Christ can bring peace on Earth. And yes, you better believe Christ can restore you. Be lifted up, be made whole by Christ, be a shining work of art that honors His greatest project—us.

Luke 2:1-5

2:1 In those days a decree went out from Emperor Augustus that all the world should be registered. 2 This was the first registration and was taken while Quirinius was governor of Syria. 3 All went to their own towns to be registered. 4 Joseph also went from the town of Nazareth in Galilee to Judea, to the city of David called Bethlehem, because he was descended from the house and family of David. 5 He went to be registered with Mary, to whom he was engaged and who was expecting a child.

I like road trips. I love to see the sights...I love the mountains, ocean, skyscrapers, or whatever's along the way. I love stopping at local restaurants and shops. Years ago we took a family trip up to the east coast to visit relatives. We would travel through fourteen states in twelve days, and planning for the trip began months in advance. I remember being really excited, mapping out the routes and seeing what landmarks were along the way. The boys were really excited as well. I think in our minds we'd imagined this grand adventure with all these fun stops to make and all will be well. The reality is that when you go through fourteen states in twelve days, you're on the road a lot. *A lot.* Being on the highway, the minutes seemed like hours, and the hours turned into days.

I remember the boys started complaining. "How much further before we stop?" Are we almost to the hotel?"

"No, we're not almost to the hotel. The hotel's in Atlanta, Georgia. We're still in Texas."

Traffic, rain, car wrecks, motion sickness, and boredom: these were the things we didn't plan on. But we finished the trip nonetheless.

Journeys seldom go exactly as planned. There's always going to be bumps in the road, things that were unexpected. Take Mary and Joseph for example. Poor Joseph. Here's a guy that's got a lot on his plate. Think about it: he finds out that his fiancé is pregnant and he's not the father. He hides the pregnancy from the public because he didn't want them to condemn her. An angel then tells him not to leave her and that his fiancé is carrying the Christ child. At the same time, the Roman Emperor Augustus mandates that every person takes part in a census, requiring every person to register themselves in their hometowns and have birth certificates recorded. The Romans didn't really care if children were legitimate or not, but the registration did provide the empire with information on how many fighting age males there were and how many families existed in what towns. This was so they could make sure that they had enough Roman soldiers in the area to quell any potential uprising against the empire, and so they had a better idea of the taxable population to fund such objectives. For Joseph and Mary, this meant leaving their quaint little town of Nazareth and traveling to Bethlehem, Joseph's ancestral hometown. Why is that a big deal? It's roughly ninety miles from Nazareth to Bethlehem...walking...with a woman who is nine months pregnant. We don't know the exact route that they took, but no matter which path they took, they took it with a woman in her third trimester. How long did this take? Well, a regular person can walk approximately twenty-four miles a day. Add a pregnant woman and probably a donkey and that number is reduced to approximately seventeen miles a day. Thus, we can assume this journey from Nazareth to Bethlehem would have lasted anywhere from five to seven days. Out in the elements, trying to conceal their identities as much as possible, these two made the journey most likely with a small group of other people. Can you imagine how these two felt? Anxiety, fear, fatigue...knowing that you are going to deliver the Christ child at any moment, but you have to travel to some far-off place to be in compliance with the law. The journey would've called for a lot of patience on their part, and trust in God. I'm quite certain that neither Joseph nor Mary had imagined things happening that way.

The path to Jesus can be one that requires patience. As much as we would like to find ourselves beside Christ, it seldom happens that way. It is not likely going to be a straight shot. There will be unexpected twists and turns, unforeseen setbacks, and it almost never happens the way we imagine it will, and it will probably take longer than we want it to. It is through the grace of God that we are led through the desert of our lives to eventually find our place with Christ. Discipleship, faith, Christianity...these are not things that we are born with or can just acquire when we decide, but rather a process, or journey if you will, that takes time. Sometimes it takes a long time. Sometimes it takes a lifetime.

Some people's journey to Christ takes longer than others. It took me a while to come around and commit myself to Christian discipleship. I would get frustrated with God, or I would find myself conflicted with doubt. Sometimes something bad or upsetting would happen in my life and it would set me back on my journey. It took me a long time to get on track for my journey to Christ, a path that I continue to travel. I pray constantly for my kids to find their path. For me, this takes a lot of patience. I feel like Joseph on that trip to Bethlehem. I just want them to be there already. But the grace and ability to await the time patiently is in us all. We might not be as close to Jesus as we want to be, there may be setbacks, but rest assured that the journey has a destination that ends with Christ.

A little over two thousand years ago, the Roman Emperor Augustus issued an edict that every person was to be registered, a process that verified people's lineage. Because of this, Joseph, having been a descendant of David, had to travel to Bethlehem with Mary, who was pregnant with Jesus. The trip lasted about seven days—it would not have been an easy trip. But what happened while Joseph and Mary were in Bethlehem would change the world forever.

Luke, 2:6-20.

2:6 While they were there, the time came for her to deliver her child. 7 And she gave birth to her firstborn son and wrapped him in bands of cloth, and laid him in a manger, because there was no place for them in the inn.

8 In that region there were shepherds living in the fields, keeping watch over their flock by night. 9 Then an angel of the Lord stood before them, and the glory of the Lord shone around them, and they were terrified. 10 But the angel said to them, "Do not be afraid; for see—I am bringing you good news of great joy for all the people: 11 to you is born this day in the city of David a Savior, who is the Messiah, the Lord. 12 This will be a sign for you: you will find a child wrapped in bands of cloth and lying in a manger." 13 And suddenly there was with the angel a multitude of the heavenly host, praising God and saying,

14 "Glory to God in the highest heaven, and on earth peace among those whom he favors!"

15 When the angels had left them and gone into heaven, the shepherds said to one another, "Let us go now to Bethlehem and see this thing that has taken place, which the Lord has made known to us." 16 So they went with haste and found Mary and Joseph, and the child lying in the manger. 17 When they saw this, they made known what had been told them about this child; 18 and all who heard it were amazed at what the shepherds told them. 19 But Mary treasured all these words and pondered them in her heart. 20 The shepherds returned, glorifying and praising God for all they had heard and seen, as it had been told them.

We live in God's world. God's world is a peaceful, happy, joyous place that we should all feel blessed to live in. Most of us won't ever know that world until our day of judgement. That's because of the chaos humanity creates for itself. Thus, we live in a chaotic world of our creation, rather than God's. Not too long ago I found myself perplexed, pondering the future of the human relationship with God. I think most of us would agree that there is far too much hatred and violence in the world. It's easy to find on social media or on the evening news. But it goes deeper than that. Each year that goes by we find that God is becoming seemingly more and more irrelevant in our chaotic world. Globally, the number of people in the world who believe in an afterlife has steadily declined at an accelerating rate. America, being built on the idea of "religious freedom" is less of a Christian stronghold. If you have a church-home that you attend, even semi-regularly, congratulations. You are now a minority. Joint-denominational research studies conducted in 2019 show that only 37% of Americans attend church. That's not just Christians, that's people of all combined faiths. The study went on to find out why people were leaving churches and religion in general. The most apparent answer was that more and more people are finding religion to be irrelevant to modern life. We live in a society where if we feel like doing something we just do it. If we want it, we just buy it. If we can't see it and touch it, we don't have to believe in it. If it doesn't fit my agenda, I'll make it fit my agenda. Just like many of the tribes of the Old Testament, the world has once again largely become a self-serving society. At one time we prayed for the things in our lives. Now we live in a world where we can engineer fetuses into a boy or a girl through medical science. We live in a world where if we need food we can just go online and order it to be delivered to our doorstep, regardless if we're in the middle of a drought or whether the livestock made it through the winter. We live in a world where our individual rights and privileges come before the word of God. We live in a world where we can dehumanize others who do not agree with us and it's perfectly acceptable. These are things that we used to pray about, things we relied on God for. Now, it's as simple as a push of a button. Artificial prayer-answering, no God required to get results. Thus, God becomes less relevant in the lives of His people. It is a sad thing.

For thirty-eight of my past thirty-nine years I have spent Christmas Eve at the Candlelight Service in the United Methodist Church. This has always been a sacred venue for me. Things are changing. Not only are we faced with division in our denomination, I can't even honestly say that small, local churches will exist at the end of my lifetime. That, too, is a sad thing.

So how can we remain relevant? If there was an obvious easy answer, smarter, more influential clergy folks than I would have already been doing it. But there is one great hope for us, and we see it most visibly during this season. It is the hope that Christ brought back into this world with His birth. A simple bundle of flesh lying wrapped up in a feeding trough, with the power and a promise to change the course of history. He is the Great Peacemaker.

One of my favorite Christmas Eve stories comes from Belgium. The year is 1914, World War I is in full swing. Many men and women, military and civilians, have died or have been wounded as a result of the conflict. On December 24th, British troops are dug into their trenches, which are covered with mud, snow, and ice. The conditions are fairly miserable in these trenches, but they are certainly a better option then up top with the crisscrossing machine gun fire and artillery from the Germans' side of the battlefield. As the British troops (Tommies) were sitting in their trenches, they could faintly hear sounds far off in the distance. Expecting an attack at any moment, they tried to make out the sounds, believing it was some sort of ploy. But to their surprise they recognized the sounds to be Christmas carols, being sung in German. With nothing better to do, the troops, who no doubt were missing spending Christmas at home with their families, began singing the songs in English.

One of the scouts who had been watching the German trenches said, "Hey, you fellows have to see this!" He handed his periscope to an officer at his side, when he peered through he saw that the Germans had placed miniature Christmas trees above the trenches and had lit candles as part of their celebration. The British troops followed suit, cutting up some evergreens and placing them on the tops of their trenches. The Germans took notice.

205

A short while later, as the singing and celebrating continued, the scout made another observation—the Germans were holding up a sign, written in broken English but clearly understandable: "You no fight, we no fight." The Brits made their own sign agreeing to what became known as the '*Flanders Christmas Eve Truce.*" But the story doesn't stop there. The troops, both British and German, left the protection of their trenches and met in the middle of the battlefield. They shook hands, swapped souvenirs with each other, and shared in food, drink, and cigarettes. As Christmas day broke, they helped each other bury their dead, prayed for one another, and then played games together. Although the fighting would commence the following day, the tradition of the Christmas Eve Truce continued throughout the duration of WWI and was later observed during certain battles in WWII.

The birth of the Christ Child was powerful enough to stop military superpowers in the midst of battle. Stories such as these should give us hope. While we find ourselves at odds with one another, and in the chaotic trenches of our lives, we must understand that these are the results of our own devices, and that Christ is more powerful than anything we can engineer ourselves. How relevant will God be to society in forty years? I can't say for certain. But I have hope. I have hope that God's grace will save us from ourselves. I have hope that Jesus will continue to work miracles in the hearts of unlikely people. I have hope that we will be brought to peace on Earth by the Great Peacemaker Himself. Let us begin our time of peace right now.

Bonus Chapter: "What's Next?"

Have you ever had one of those days where you had a whole list of things to do, and then you finished them and didn't know what to do next? It reminds me of a dog that used to live down my road. Every day when I would leave for work, the dog would bark and run full-speed behind me trying to catch me. On the way home, it was the same thing: the dog runs out to the side of the road, barks, and chases me as fast he could until he eventually tired out and gave up. This was a daily regiment for a couple years. One day, being the mature, sophisticated man that I am, I pondered what the dog might do if it actually caught my truck. At that moment I hit the brakes and slid to a stop. The dog did too. He just stood there beside my truck, standing in the ditch with a perplexed look on his face. He didn't rip my tire to shreds, he didn't leap through the window to get me. He just stood there with a confused look on his face. He had finally reached a new level of this game, but he didn't know what to do next. Not unlike the dog, there was a point in my life where I was dealing with a lot of stuff and chasing Jesus to make it all better, but then things got better and I didn't know what I was supposed to do next. Surely this wasn't all there was to it. I knew there were still some hard times ahead. I knew Jesus was going to walk with me through those hard times. But is that all?

Of course not! If that was the case we would celebrate Christmas, celebrate the birth of Christ, and just stop there, because Jesus made things better, no need to go on. But that's not what happened. In fact, right after Jesus' birth things got pretty intense.

Matthew 2:13-23

2:13 Now after they had left, an angel of the Lord appeared to Joseph in a dream and said, "Get up, take the child and his mother, and flee to Egypt, and remain there until I tell you; for Herod is about to search for the child, to destroy him." 14 Then Joseph got up, took the child and his mother by night, and went to Egypt, 15 and remained there until the death of Herod. This was to fulfill what had been spoken by the Lord through the prophet, "Out of Egypt I have called my son."

16 When Herod saw that he had been tricked by the wise men, he was infuriated, and he sent and killed all the children in and around Bethlehem who were two years old or under, according to the time that he had learned from the wise men. 17 Then was fulfilled what had been spoken through the prophet Jeremiah:

18 "A voice was heard in Ramah,

  wailing and loud lamentation,

Rachel weeping for her children;

  she refused to be consoled, because they are no more."

19 When Herod died, an angel of the Lord suddenly appeared in a dream to Joseph in Egypt and said, 20 "Get up, take the child and his mother, and go to the land of Israel, for those who were seeking the child's life are dead." 21 Then Joseph got up, took the child and his mother, and went to the land of Israel. 22 But when he heard that Archelaus was ruling over Judea in place of his father Herod, he was afraid to go there. And after being warned in a dream, he went away to the district of Galilee. 23 There he made his home in a town called Nazareth, so that what had been spoken through the prophets might be fulfilled, "He will be called a Nazorean."

Now, I doubt very highly that Joseph and Mary had planned on being hunted by Herod, or fleeing to Egypt. It happened nonetheless. It wasn't the way they had imagined it. But what a great testimony they gained out of the situation: putting themselves on the line to protect baby Jesus, doing their part to fulfill the prophecy.

So here we are: Jesus Christ has entered into our lives as our Savior. We set out to seek Him, and we have found Him. And we don't just stop there. Now is not the time to stop and stand there with a confused look on your face. In case you haven't realized it yet, the story of Christ and salvation through grace is a continuous story that goes on infinitely.

So, it took me a while to realize what the next steps were. Some of my parishioners have remarked on the fact that I use a lot of personal illustrations in my sermon lessons, things that are unique to me and the way Christ has touched my life. And while I might sound like any other storyteller, what I'm actually doing is sharing my testimony with the world to glorify the amazing power of Christ. You see, the Holy Bible ends with the Book of Revelations, but the story of Jesus Christ is one that keeps going and going and going. You and I both have our stories, our chapters, to write. Our struggles, our victories, our sorrows, our faith—all are part of the Jesus story. Not only must we not be afraid to share those testimonies with others, we must not be afraid to live them. It is in these times that the greatest stories of Christ in our lives are written. Trust that He will co-author them with you every step of the way.

Conclusion

Our faith is unique to us. The words on these preceding pages are unique to my faith, and I wish to share them with the world. The other unique characteristic about fingerprints is that they leave an impression, an imprint, long after the one who placed it has gone. While these imprints have been key pieces of evidence in solving millions of crimes over the years, the imprint of one's faith is no less important. I cannot begin to count all the people whose faith experiences, insights, and interpretations have helped navigate my journey to Christ. No matter who you are, no matter where you came from, know that your faith is yours *because* of those experiences. And it is sacred.

About the Author

Ashley (Ash) David Harmon was born in Dallas, Texas in 1980. He is a veteran law enforcement officer now serving as a deputy constable for Collin County, Texas, and police instructor at Collin College. He is also a fifth-generation Methodist minister, currently appointed as the Senior Pastor of two churches in the North Texas Conference of the United Methodist Church. An avid outdoorsman, Ash enjoys hiking, hunting, mountain climbing, and sports. He resides in the Dallas area of north Texas.

Made in the USA
Coppell, TX
04 November 2020

40757111R00118